Ian McEwan

ECl

D1347119

NEW BRITISH FICTION

Series editors:
Philip Tew
Rod Mengham

Published
Sonya Andermahr: **Jeanette Winterson**
Bradley Buchanan: **Hanif Kureishi**
Frederick M. Holmes: **Julian Barnes**
Kaye Mitchell: **A. L. Kennedy**
Robert Morace: **Irvine Welsh**
Stephen Morton: **Salman Rushdie**
Mark Rawlinson: **Pat Barker**
Philip Tew: **Zadie Smith**
Lynn Wells: **Ian McEwan**

Forthcoming
Gerard Barrett: **Graham Swift**
Sebastian Groes: **Martin Amis**
Rod Mengham: **Jonathan Coe**
Mark Wormald: **Kazuo Ishiguro**

New British Fiction Series
Series Standing Order

ISBN 1–4039–4274–9 hardback
ISBN 1–4039–4275–7 paperback
(*outside North America only*)

You can receive future titles in this series as they are published by placing a standing order. Please contact your bookseller or, in the case of difficulty, write to us at the address below with your name and address, the title of the series and the ISBN quoted above.

Customer Services Department, Palgrave Ltd
Houndmills, Basingstoke, Hampshire RG21 6XS, England

NEW BRITISH FICTION

Ian McEwan

Lynn Wells

palgrave
macmillan

First published 2010 by
PALGRAVE MACMILLAN

Palgrave Macmillan in the UK is an imprint of Macmillan Publishers Limited, registered in England, company number 785998, of Houndmills, Basingstoke, Hampshire RG21 6XS.

Palgrave Macmillan in the US is a division of St Martin's Press LLC, 175 Fifth Avenue, New York, NY 10010.

Palgrave Macmillan is the global academic imprint of the above companies and has companies and representatives throughout the world.

Palgrave® and Macmillan® are registered trademarks in the United States, the United Kingdom, Europe and other countries.

ISBN-13: 978–1–4039–8781–5 hardback
ISBN-13: 978–1–4039–8782–2 paperback

This book is printed on paper suitable for recycling and made from fully managed and sustained forest sources. Logging, pulping and manufacturing processes are expected to conform to the environmental regulations of the country of origin.

A catalogue record for this book is available from the British Library.

A catalog record for this book is available from the Library of Congress.

10   9   8   7   6   5   4   3   2   1
19   18   17   16   15   14   13   12   11   10

Printed and bound in China

CONTENTS

GENERAL EDITORS' PREFACE

This series highlights with its very title two crucial elements in the nature of contemporary British fiction, especially as a field for academic research and study. The first term indicates the originality and freshness of such writing expressed in a huge formal diversity. The second evokes the cultural identity of the authors included, who nevertheless represent through their diversity a challenge to any hegemonic or narrow view of Britishness. As regards the fiction, many of the writers featured in this series continue to draw from and adapt long traditions of cultural and aesthetic practice. Such aesthetic continuities contrast starkly with the conditions of knowledge at the end of the twentieth century and the beginning of the twenty-first, a period that has been characterized by an apprehension of radical presentness, a sense of unprecedented forms of experience and an obsession with new modes of self-awareness. This stage of the survival of the novel may perhaps be best remembered as a millennial and post-millennial moment, a time of fluctuating reading practices and of historical events whose impact is largely still unresolved. The new fiction of these times reflects a rapidly changing cultural and ideological reality, as well as a renewal of the commitment of both writers and readers to both the relevance and utility of narrative forms of knowledge.

Each volume in this series will serve as an introductory guide to an individual author chosen from a list of those whose work has proved to be of general interest to reviewers, academics, students and the general reading public. Each volume will offer information concerning the life, work and literary and cultural contexts appropriate to the chosen subject of each book; individual volumes will share the same overall structure with a largely common organization of materials. The result is intended to be suitable for both academic and general readers: putting accessibility at a premium, without compromising an ambitious series of readings of today's most vitally interesting British novelists, interpreting their work, assessing their influences, and exploring their relationship to the times in which they live.

Philip Tew and Rod Mengham

PREFACE

This book forms part of Palgrave Macmillan's *New British Fiction Series*, and I am grateful to the publisher and the series editors for this opportunity to conduct a comprehensive study of one of England's most celebrated authors. While I refer to works from across Ian McEwan's career, I give special attention to some of his most famous novels—*The Child in Time, Enduring Love, Atonement* and *Saturday*—which reward the critic with many complexities of narrative form and textual detail. The focus that I have chosen to bring McEwan's oeuvre is on ethical relationships, both within the texts themselves and between the author and world in which he lives. While moral philosophy offers many ideas applicable to literary analysis, the writings of Emmanuel Lévinas for me have an immediate affinity to McEwan's work, particularly in the image of the face-to-face encounter. In addition to drawing on Lévinas, I deploy a wide range of theoretical models and critical sources that illuminate the fiction in new ways. This study is meant to be "critical" in the best sense of that word; although it sometimes raises difficult questions about McEwan's writing, I believe it does so in a spirit of respect for a talented artist with an ethical stake in the human endeavour.

ACKNOWLEDGEMENTS

I would like to thank the series editors, Dr Philip Tew and Dr Rod Mengham, and the editorial team at Palgrave Macmillan, UK—Kitty van Boxel, Sonya Barker, Felicity Noble and Kate Wallis, as well as my project manager Cherline Daniel at Integra—for their professionalism and patience, and for giving me the opportunity to publish this book. I would also like to thank Todd Bryanton for his work on the index. The Humanities Research Institute and the Faculty of Arts at the University of Regina provided financial support without which this project would have never seen completion. I am grateful to Mr McEwan for welcoming me into his home for an interview in December 2005, and for generously giving his time to editing the transcript. A special thanks to the students in my senior seminar on McEwan's work at the University of Regina in 2008, who asked many hard questions and spurred my imagination.

The largest debt of gratitude goes to my family—my husband Brian Johnson; our four children, Annie, Jesse, Ted and Erin; and my parents, Ben and Lillian Wells—who kept faith with me over the years and helped me immensely.

LIST OF ABBREVIATIONS

PART I
Introduction

TIMELINE

1960   Harold Macmillan "Winds of Change" speech, Cape Town, South Africa
John F. Kennedy elected as US President
Aged six, Kazuo Ishiguro arrives in Britain

1961   Adolf Eichmann on trial in Israel for role in Holocaust
Bay of Pigs: attempted invasion of Cuba
Berlin Wall constructed
Yuri Gagarin first person in Space
Silicon chip patented
Private Eye magazine begins publication
Muriel Spark, *The Prime of Miss Jean Brodie*
Jonathan Coe born

1962   Cuban Missile Crisis
Marilyn Monroe dies
Independence for Uganda; followed this decade by Kenya (1963), Northern Rhodesia (1964), Southern Rhodesia (1965), Barbados (1966)

1963   John F. Kennedy assassinated in Dallas
Martin Luther King Jr delivers "I Have a Dream" speech
Profumo Affair

1964   Nelson Mandela sentenced to life imprisonment
Commercial pirate radio challenges BBC monopoly

1965   State funeral of Winston Churchill
US sends troops to Vietnam
A. L. Kennedy born in Dundee, Scotland

1966   Ian Brady and Myra Hindley sentenced to life imprisonment for Moors Murders
England beats West Germany 4–2 at Wembley to win Football World Cup
Star Trek series debut on NBC television
Jean Rhys, *The Wide Sargasso Sea*

1967   Six-Day War in the Middle East
World's first heart transplant
Abortion Act legalizes termination of pregnancy in UK
Sergeant Pepper's Lonely Hearts Club Band album released by The Beatles
Flann O'Brien, *The Third Policeman*

1968   Anti-Vietnam War protestors attempt to storm American Embassy in Grosvenor Square
Martin Luther King Jr assassinated
Robert F. Kennedy assassinated
Student protests and riots in France
Lord Chamberlain's role as censor of plays in the UK is abolished
Lindsay Anderson, *If . . .*

1969   Civil rights march in Northern Ireland attacked by Protestants
Apollo 11 lands on the Moon with Neil Armstrong's famous first steps
Rock concert at Woodstock
Yasser Arafat becomes leader of PLO
Booker Prize first awarded; winner P. H. Newby, *Something to Answer for*
Open University founded in the UK
John Fowles, *The French Lieutenant's Woman*

1970   Popular Front for the Liberation of Palestine (PFLP) hijacks five planes
Students activists and bystanders shot in anti-Vietnam War protest at Kent State University, Ohio, four killed, nine wounded
UK voting age reduced from 21 years to 18 years

1971   Decimal currency introduced in the UK
Internment without trial of terrorist suspects in Northern Ireland begins
India and Pakistan in conflict after Bangladesh declares independence

1972   Miners' strike
Bloody Sunday in Londonderry, 14 protestors killed outright or fatally wounded by British troops
Aldershot barracks bomb initiates IRA campaign with seven dead
Britain enters Common Market
Massacre of Israeli athletes at Munich Olympics
Watergate scandal
Anthony Burgess, *A Clockwork Orange*
Samuel Beckett, *Not I*

1973   US troops leave Vietnam
Arab–Israeli 15-day Yom Kippur War
PM Edward Heath introduces three-day working week
Martin Amis, *The Rachel Papers*

1974   Miners' strike
IRA bombings in Guildford (five dead) and Birmingham (21 dead)

1975   Microsoft founded
Sex Discrimination Act
Zadie Smith born in North London
Malcolm Bradbury, *The History Man*
Ian McEwan, *First Love, Last Rites*, which wins the Somerset Maugham Award in 1976

1976 Weak economy forces UK government loan from the International Monetary Fund (IMF)
Ian McEwan, *First Love, Last Rites*

1977 *Star Wars* released
UK unemployment tops 1,600,000
Nintendo begins to sell computer games
Sex Pistols "Anarchy in the UK" tour

1978 Soviet troops occupy Afghanistan
First test-tube baby born in Oldham, England
Ian McEwan, *In Between the Sheets* and *The Cement Garden*

1979 Iranian Revolution establishes Islamic theocracy
Margaret Thatcher becomes PM after Conservative election victory
USSR invades Afghanistan
Lord Mountbatten assassinated by the IRA

1980 Iran–Iraq War starts
Iranian Embassy siege in London
CND rally at Greenham Common airbase, England
IRA hunger strike at Belfast Maze Prison over political status for prisoners
Julian Barnes, *Metroland*

1981 Prince Charles and Lady Diana marry in St Paul's Cathedral with 750 million worldwide television audience
Widespread urban riots in UK including in Brixton, Holloway, Toxteth, Handsworth, Moss Side
AIDS identified
First IBM personal computer
Alasdair Gray, *Lanark*
Salman Rushdie, *Midnight's Children*, which wins Booker Prize for Fiction
Ian McEwan, *The Comfort of Strangers*

1982 Mark Thatcher, PM's son, disappears for three days in Sahara during the Paris-Dakar rally
Falklands War with Argentina, costing the UK over £1.6 billion

Body of Roberto Calvi, chairman of Vatican-connected Banco Ambrosiano, found hanging beneath Blackfriars Bridge, London

1983   Klaus Barbie, Nazi war criminal, arrested in Bolivia
Beirut: US Embassy and barracks bombing, killing hundreds of members of multinational peacekeeping force, mostly US marines
US troops invade Grenada
Microsoft Word first released
Salman Rushdie, *Shame*, which wins Prix du Meilleur Livre Etranger (France)

1984   Miners' strike
HIV identified as cause of AIDS
IRA bomb at Conservative Party Conference in Brighton kills four
British Telecom privatization shares sale
Thirty-eight deaths during clashes at Liverpool v. Juventus football match at Heysel Stadium, Brussels
Martin Amis, *Money: A Suicide Note*
Julian Barnes, *Flaubert's Parrot*
James Kelman, *Busconductor Hines*
Graham Swift, *Waterland*

1985   Famine in Ethiopia and Live Aid concert
Damage to ozone layer discovered
Mikhail Gorbachev becomes Soviet Premier and introduces *glasnost* (openness with the West) and *perestroika* (economic restructuring)
PC Blakelock murdered during riots on Broadwater Farm estate in Tottenham, London
My Beautiful Laundrette film released (dir. Stephen Frears, screenplay Hanif Kureishi)
Jeanette Winterson, *Oranges Are Not the Only Fruit*

1986   Abolition of Greater London Council and other metropolitan county councils in England
Violence between police and protestors at Wapping, East London after Rupert Murdoch sacks 5000 print workers

Challenger shuttle explodes
Chernobyl nuclear accident
US bombs Libya
Peter Ackroyd, *Hawksmoor*

1987 Capsizing of RORO ferry, *Herald of Free Enterprise*, off Zee-brugge kills 193 people
London Stock Exchange and market collapse on "Black Monday"
Remembrance Sunday: eleven killed by Provisional IRA bomb in Enniskillen
Ian McEwan, *The Child in Time*, which wins Whitbread Novel Award in 1987 and the Prix Fémina Etranger in 1993
Jeanette Winterson, *The Passion*

1988 US shoots down Iranian passenger flight
Pan Am flight 103 bombed over Lockerbie, 270 people killed
Soviet troop withdrawals from Afghanistan begin
Salman Rushdie, *The Satanic Verses*

1989 Fatwa issued against Rushdie by Iranian leadership (Khomeini)
Fall of Berlin Wall
Exxon Valdez oil disaster
Student protestors massacred in Tiananmen Square, Bejing
Hillsborough Stadium disaster in which 96 football fans die
Kazuo Ishiguro, *The Remains of the Day*, which wins Booker Prize for Fiction
Jeanette Winterson, *Sexing the Cherry*

1990 London poll tax riots
Fall of Thatcher; John Major becomes Conservative PM
Nelson Mandela freed from jail
Jeanette Winterson adapts *Oranges* for BBC television film
A. S. Byatt, *Possession*
Hanif Kureishi, *The Buddha of Suburbia*, which wins Whitbread First Novel Prize
A. L. Kennedy, *Night Geometry and the Garscadden Trains*

1991 Soviet Union collapses
First Iraq War with 12-day Operation Desert Storm
Apartheid ended in South Africa
PM Major negotiates opt-out for Britain from European Monetary Union and rejects Social Chapter of Maastricht Treaty
Hypertext Markup Language (HTML) helps create the World Wide Web
Hanif Kureishi: screenplays for *Sammy and Rosie Get Laid* and *London Kills Me*
Pat Barker, *Regeneration*

1992 "Black Wednesday" stock market crisis when UK forced to exit European Exchange Rate Mechanism
Adam Thorpe, *Ulverton*

1993 Black teenager Stephen Lawrence murdered in Well Hall Road, London
With Downing Street Declaration, PM John Major and Taoiseach Albert Reynolds commit Britain and Ireland to joint Northern Ireland resolution
Film of Ishiguro's *The Remains of the Day*, starring Anthony Hopkins and Emma Thompson
Irvine Welsh, *Trainspotting*
Ian McEwan, *Black Dogs*

1994 Tony Blair elected leader of Labour Party following death of John Smith
Channel Tunnel opens
Nelson Mandela elected President of South Africa
Provisional IRA and loyalist paramilitary cease-fire
Homosexual age of consent for men in the UK lowered to 18
Mike Newell (dir.), *Four Weddings and a Funeral*
Jonathan Coe, *What a Carve Up!*
James Kelman, *How late it was, how late*, which wins Booker Prize for Fiction
Irvine Welsh, *The Acid House*

1995 Oklahoma City bombing
Srebrenica massacre during Bosnian War

Pat Barker, *The Ghost Road*
Nicholas Hytner (dir.), *The Madness of King George*
Hanif Kureishi, *The Black Album*

1996 Cases of Bovine Spongeiform Encephalitis (Mad Cow Disease) in the UK
Divorce of Charles and Diana
Breaching cease-fire, Provisional IRA bombs London's Canary Wharf and Central Manchester
Film of Irvine Welsh's *Trainspotting* (dir. Danny Boyle), starring Ewan McGregor and Robert Carlyle
Graham Swift, *Last Orders*, which wins Booker Prize

1997 Tony Blair becomes Labour PM after landslide victory
Princess Diana dies in Paris car crash
Hong Kong returned to China by UK
Jim Crace, *Quarantine*
Jonathan Coe, *The House of Sleep*, which wins Prix Médicis Etranger (France)
Ian McEwan, *Enduring Love*
Iain Sinclair and Marc Atkins, *Lights Out for the Territory*

1998 Good Friday Agreement on Northern Ireland and Northern Ireland Assembly established
Twenty-eight people killed by splinter group Real IRA bombing in Omagh
Sonny Bono Act extends copyright to lifetime plus 70 years
BFI/Channel 4 film *Stella Does Tricks*, released (screenplay A. L. Kennedy)
Julian Barnes, *England, England*
Ian McEwan, *Amsterdam*, which wins the Booker Prize

1999 Euro currency adopted
Macpherson Inquiry into Stephen Lawrence murder accuses London's Metropolitan Police of institutional racism
NATO bombs Serbia over Kosovo crisis
Welsh Assembly and Scottish Parliament both open
Thirty-one passengers killed in Ladbroke Grove train disaster

2000   Anti-globalization protest and riots in London
Hauliers and farmers blockade oil refineries in fuel price
protest in the UK
Kazuo Ishiguro, *When We Were Orphans*
Will Self, *How the Dead Live*
Zadie Smith, *White Teeth*
Ian McEwan awarded CBE

2001   9/11 Al-Qaeda attacks on World Trade Center and Pen-
tagon
Bombing and invasion of Afghanistan
Riots in Oldham, Leeds, Bradford, and Burnley, Northern
England
Labour Party under Blair re-elected to government
Ian McEwan, *Atonement*, which wins the W. H. Smith Lit-
erary Award in 2002, the National Book Critics' Circle
Fiction Award in 2003, the L.A. Times Prize for Fiction
in 2003, and the Santiago Prize for the European Novel in
2004

2002   Queen Mother dies aged 101
Rowan Williams named next Archbishop of Canterbury
Bali terrorist bomb kills 202 people and injures a further
209
Inquiry concludes English general practitioner Dr Harold
Shipman killed around 215 patients
Zadie Smith's *White Teeth* adapted for Channel 4 television
broadcast in autumn

2003   Invasion of Iraq and fall of Saddam Hussein
Death of UK government scientist Dr David Kelly, and
Hutton Inquiry
Worldwide threat of Severe Acute Respiratory Syndrome
(SARS)

2004   BBC Director General Greg Dyke steps down over Kelly
affair
Bombings in Madrid kill 190 people and injure over 1700
Expansion of NATO to include seven ex-Warsaw Pact
countries

European Union expands to 25 countries as eight ex-communist states join

Jonathan Coe, *Like a Fiery Elephant: The Story of B. S. Johnson*

Alan Hollinghurst, *The Line of Beauty*, which wins Booker Prize for Fiction

Andrea Levy, *Small Island*, which wins Orange Prize for Fiction

Film release of *Enduring Love* (dir. Roger Michell)

2005 UK ban on foxhunting with dogs comes into force

7/7 London suicide bombings on transport system kill 52 and injure over 700 commuters in morning rush hour

Hurricane Katrina kills at least 1836 people and floods devastate New Orleans

After four failed bombings are detected, Brazilian Jean Charles de Menezes is shot and killed by Metropolitan Police officers at Stockwell Underground Station

Ian McEwan, *Saturday*, which wins the James Tait Black Memorial Prize in 2006

Zadie Smith, *On Beauty*, which wins 2006 Orange Prize for Fiction

2006 Jeanette Winterson awarded the OBE

Airline terror plot thwarted, causes major UK airline delays

Israel–Hezbollah war in Lebanon

Five prostitutes killed in Ipswich in a six-week period

Saddam Hussein executed by hanging in controversial circumstances

2007 Ian McEwan, *On Chesil Beach*, which is named the Galaxy Book of the Year at the 2008 British Book Awards

Film release of *Atonement* (dir. Joe Wright), which wins Oscars and Golden Globes in 2008

1

INTRODUCTION

It is hard to dispute that Ian McEwan has evolved as a writer, adopting different styles and genres to suit the ideas and situations he finds most urgently in need of expression; becoming more openly sophisticated about the power of narrative to communicate, to reconcile and at times to deceive; and writing prose that gains him international respect for its technical beauty, emotional timbre and intellectual depth. Once considered, along with his friend Martin Amis, one of the *enfants terribles* of the British literary scene, he is now touted by many, such as this reviewer, as the best writer of contemporary fiction in English in the world: "McEwan is not only the greatest living writer in England; now that Bellow has stopped writing, and now that Roth's mastery of le mot juste has exploded . . . McEwan is writing better English prose than anybody. The Nobel Prize committee could start making itself respectable by giving him the nod" (Siegel 4).

The commonly accepted explanation for McEwan's rise to the pinnacle of contemporary authorship is that he has, in effect, "grown up", leaving behind the grotesque fantasies, sexual violence and freakish outsider characters, many of whom are children or adolescents, of his early fiction, which had earned him the nickname "Ian Macabre." After a number of years as, in his own words, "the chronicler of comically exaggerated psychopathic states of mind or of adolescent anxiety, snot and pimples" (Haffenden 173), McEwan took a hiatus from fiction in the 1980s; during this time, which he devoted to writing in other forms such as screenplays and an oratorio, he executed what Claudia Schemberg calls an "ethical turn" in his work, "openly engaging in complex ethical, social and historical issues" (28) and transforming himself into "a social or moral prophet" (29). From his return to fiction in 1987 with *The Child in Time*, he committed himself to writing about the sorts of mature social, historical and political themes thought to be more properly the province of the serious novelist. While his texts from the late 1980s onwards deal with a wide range of subject matters and are written in a variety of generic forms, with the exception of *Enduring Love* (1997) and *On Chesil Beach* (2007), which return to a focus on intimate relationships, they reveal a political dimension unseen in his earlier work.

Central to this view of McEwan's evolution is the belief in the concomitant refinement of his ethical sensibility; David Malcolm, in his study, states with confidence, "Overall, McEwan's career shows a trajectory from quite extreme moral relativism toward a clear moral focus" (15). Malcolm's assessment seems justifiable when we contrast the apparent amorality of an early story such as "Butterflies", in which the first-person narrator reveals no remorse for having sexually assaulted and murdered a child, with the clearly articulated positions of the physician Henry Perowne and his artistic children Daisy and Theo for and against the 2003 invasion of Iraq in *Saturday* (2005), one of McEwan's most recent books. But as critics Head and Kiernan Ryan before him have pointed out, "the simple narrative of linear development" (Head 7) behind this "moral fable" about the author "who grows out of his nasty adolescent fantasies and into a responsible adult novelist" (Ryan 1994: 2) needs to be closely scrutinized—as is only suitable in the context of a writer who himself is highly self-conscious about how narratives work to convey meaning. In my view, it is crucial to consider carefully the complex relationship between the depiction of moral issues in McEwan's work and the specific aesthetic construction—in terms of genre, narrative structure and voice—of each text. As we shall see, these sorts of analyses, for which I draw on a wide range of theoretical models and ideas in the chapters to come, do not support unconditionally the argument that McEwan has grown in a straight line from a kind of artistic infancy to an eminent maturity, but rather that, at times, his growing sophistication as a writer has rendered his moral vision both more complex and more problematic.

The dark, often lurid nature of McEwan's early fiction earned him a reputation for grotesqueness and amorality that would stay with him for many years. His first two publications, the short story collections *First Love, Last Rites* (1975) and *In Between the Sheets* (1978), are populated with freakish and outcast characters living in degraded urban environments where mutilation, murder and sexual violence are commonplace. Evident in this early work is McEwan's growing interest in feminism, to which he was exposed first when he read Germaine Greer's *The Female Eunuch* in 1971. The stories abound with unsavoury male types who objectify and dominate women, including a man who becomes infatuated with a department store mannequin, which he eventually "murders" in a sexual rage. But as Malcolm notes, the female characters in McEwan's stories "are often far from admirable themselves" (14), including two women who emasculate their philandering mutual male lover.

Gender dynamics have continued to play a key role throughout McEwan's career. In the 1982 oratio "Or Shall We Die?", inspired by the threat of nuclear holocaust, McEwan has a female voice articulate the values of environmental stewardship, peaceful coexistence and care for children, while the male voice is aggressive, militaristic and bent on conquest. The figures of the domineering male and the victimized female reappear in *The Comfort of Strangers* (1981) and *The Innocent* (1990), while in other texts such as *The Child in Time* (1987), *Black Dogs* (1993) and *Enduring Love* (1997), women are associated with the positive term of various binaristic relationships—between art and science, spirtualism and materialism, irrationality and reason. Over the years, McEwan has moved away from these rather clichéd conceptions of the masculine and feminine, as he explained in 2008 to *Times* reporter Richard Morrison: "In 1982 I had the rather romantic notion—which many writers hold at some point or another—that the problem with the world is actually men, and that everything would be all right if women ran it. I no longer hold that view" (2). In recent novels such as *Atonement* (2001) and *Saturday*, the often one-dimensional feminist approach of the early work has given way to more nuanced depictions of male/female interactions.

In all of McEwan's texts, issues of gender are central to his representation of ethical relationships. As Jessica Benjamin argues in *The Bonds of Love: Psychoanalysis, Feminism, and the Problem of Domination*, the divisions between men and women, the products of historical forces of ignorance and inequality, illuminate the inherent difficulty of recognizing the other as separate, yet bound to the self through shared needs and desires:

> Real recognition of the other entails being able to perceive commonality through difference; and true differentiation sustains the balance between separateness and connection in a dynamic tension. But once identification with the other is denied, love becomes only the love of an object, of The Other .... Loss of mutual recognition is the most common consequence of gender polarity. (171)

Benjamin's ideas about the need for recognition of the other's distinctness yet integral connection with the self in the context of gender relations has affinities with the ethical philosophy of French thinker Emmanuel Lévinas (1906–1995). For Lévinas, a Jew who was a prisoner of war from 1940 to 1945, ethics is "first philosophy" (Hand 76); he rejected the ontological metaphysics of Martin Heidegger, which focus on individual being, in favour of an intersubjective understanding of human relations. According to Lévinas, while we can never know other people in their entirety since they are inherently different from us, we exist in a state of "indebtedness" to them for our identity, as Tim Woods points out: "One's sense of self derives from turning to another, and the self is thus always divided, always finding its source elsewhere" (56, 53). We therefore have a natural responsibility to care for others, on whom our very existences depend; this essentially altruistic relationship forms the "precondition for being" (Woods 53), the moral foundation that makes society possible. As I will discuss in Chapter 5, the failure to recognize the needs of others as separate beings on a grand scale results in totalitarianism and violence such as that experienced during the Second World War.

Lévinas's image for the compassionate acknowledgement of alterity is the face: "To be in relation with the other face-to-face— is to be unable to kill" (*Entre Nous* 10). What the face represents is not the power implied by various social roles, but the utter vulnerability of the being in the world: "The absolute nakedness of a face, the absolutely defenseless face, without covering, clothing or mask, is what opposes my power over it, my violence" (Lévinas, *Collected Philosophical Papers* 21). In the truly ethical relationship, the other's weakness "summons" us to responsibility and caring, without expectation of reciprocation, even "to the point of dying for the other" (*Entre Nous* 147, 173).

Since his "ethical turn" in the 1980s, McEwan's fiction has been most acute in its examination of elemental ethics in its depictions of literal face-to-face encounters, moments when he pits individual characters against one another at crucial points of decision during which they must choose between self-gratification, or even self-preservation, and genuine benevolent action. These scenarios—Stephen Lewis's altercations with a beggar girl in *The Child in Time*, Jeremy's confrontation with an abusive father in *Black Dogs*, Joe's decision whether to hold onto a hot-air balloon rope in *Enduring Love*, the composer Clive's choice between his art and heroism in *Amsterdam* (1998), the adolescent Briony's accusation of Robbie in *Atonement*, Henry's clashes with the thug Baxter in *Saturday*—serve as internal mirrors of the basic ethical relationship as framed by Lévinas in his philosophy. As Lévinas notes, the failure to recognize one's responsibility for others is the first step towards violence and oppression, and McEwan frequently uses the characters in these dramatic encounters as object lessons of the negative consequences that come with choosing self-interest over caring for the other.

By concentrating the act of ethical decision making in these dramatic scenes, McEwan creates clear points of identification for his readers, who must bring their own sense of judgement to the situations. The self-consciousness of these key encounters thus extends beyond the texts themselves, as readers are induced to reflect upon the values underlying their own dealings with others. As Wayne Booth suggests in *The Company We Keep: An Ethics of Fiction*, the process of reading involves our experience of the "full 'otherness' " (136) of the author's work from us, both as a textual object *per se* and as the representation of lives separate from ours. Schemberg, drawing on Booth's work, explains how fiction, since it "does not entail any direct practical choice for the *self* in the 'real' world of social interaction," provides a safe medium for readerly reflection, "a fertile testing ground for (moral) ideas" (23). With their emphasis on dramatic interactions between characters, McEwan's mid-career and recent novels highlight the role that fiction can play in soliciting our imaginative understanding of others, and in enacting for our consideration the vicarious challenge of behaving towards them with genuine compassion.

But while McEwan was integrating scenes of intense ethical reflection into his later fiction, at the same time he was experimenting more with textual self-consciousness, which reached its apotheosis with the multi-layered, highly allusive *Atonement*. In our interview, McEwan said of that novel, "If it appears to be 'intertextual' or 'self-referencing' that is only because my head is stuffed with the pleasures of reading" (see page 126–7); and it is no coincidence that the most passionate scene of lovemaking he has ever written takes place in a library. Like many writers coming of age in the 1980s, McEwan was strongly influenced by the postmodernist techniques of contemporary novelists such as Iris Murdoch and John Fowles in England. As Linda Hutcheon outlines in her influential study *A Poetics of Postmodernism* (1988), contemporary writers from the 1960s onwards, cognizant of the ideas of poststructuralist theory about the limits of using language to represent reality, were building self-reflexivity into their works, deliberately disrupting the realist illusion and calling attention to the fictiveness of their books using a number of strategies: the embedding within their novels of authorial and other artistic figures, as well as acts of storytelling and interpretation, which reflect on the creative process behind the text at hand and its relationship with its readers; the inclusion of thematic passages to do with the power and stability of language; the use of overt intertextuality, generic imitations and parody, which emphasize the constructedness of their narratives; experimentation with different kinds of narrative voices, particularly those whose deceptiveness or reliability challenge the readers to play an active hermeneutic role; and a particular focus on the representation of history that reveals its similarities to literary fiction.

With openly self-conscious texts set in the past such as *The Innocent*, *Black Dogs* and *Atonement*, McEwan has established himself as one of the world's foremost writers of "historiographic metafiction," to borrow Hutcheon's term; while recognizing that history can never be fully represented in language, he tests the limits of our ability to represent and understand it, as Tim S. Gauthier notes, "McEwan exhibits a paradoxical relationship with the past. He knows that it cannot be known, but this does not prevent him from trying to know it" (23). He is equally complex in his attitude towards textual self-consciousness in general:

I sometimes feel that every sentence contains a ghostly commentary on its own processes. This is not always helpful, but I don't think you can ever quite escape it. At best, you can take it for granted, and not become enslaved to self-reference, and remain faithful to the sensuous, telepathic capabilities of language as it transfers thoughts and feelings from one person's mind to another. (Begley 59)

Despite his acknowledgement of the inevitability of self-reflexive aspects in his work, McEwan remains confident that his fiction can produce, through the creation of believable characters and compellingly readable narratives in the tradition of the great English novelists, the imaginative conditions for entering into the minds of others and achieving greater moral awareness.

The increasing literariness of his works is paralleled by his refinement of narrative technique, which he links specifically to his wish to make possible imaginative entry into the minds of others, central to his conception of morality. In our interview, he noted that, until the early 1980s, he "was more interested in surfaces," adding that he "thought it was almost cheating to let the reader know what a character was thinking" (see page 126). By the time he returned to fiction in 1987, he was tired of this kind of exteriorized narration of events, which he saw as a "dead aesthetic" (XX), and worked instead to create a narrative form that could be used to "represent consciousness, the flow of thought, to give an interior narrative, a subjective history of an individual through time, through every conceivable event, through love, crises or moral dilemmas" (XX).

In order to make possible this degree of access to his characters' minds, McEwan had to become adept at creating modes of third-person narration that can move seamlessly from one perspective to another, while allowing for narratorial commentary. For example, when the narrator of *Saturday* asserts, "Naturally, Theo is against the war in Iraq" (151), it is not clear whether the opinion is Henry's, McEwan's, or that of some generalized societal voice. The deftness of this sort of narratorial sleight of hand wins McEwan considerable critical praise, but it also poses an additional challenge to us as readers: what position is this text asking us to identify with? Are we expected to agree automatically with the narrator's presumption about the political views of artistic young men? Or is there an "edge," to borrow Linda Hutcheon's term (1994), of irony built up, subtly and cumulatively, by such narratorial gestures, that we as readers should detect and scrutinize?

The interaction between McEwan's evolving literary techniques and his presentation of moral issues, particularly through those dramatic scenes of ethical encounter, forms the basis of the analyses of his work in the chapters that follow. Following the biographical reading, I briefly examine in Chapter 3 his first two novels *The Cement Garden* and *The Comfort of Strangers*, in terms of their depiction of relationships based on domination among individuals in intimate, often claustrophobic, environments. The characters in these early experimental works are largely on the fringe of normal adult society—orphaned children, lost tourists—who are caught up in their own desires or are objectified by others.

Chapter 4 is entirely devoted to McEwan's first major novel, *The Child in Time*, set in an imaginary London of the near future during the reign of an oppressive right-wing government, clearly based on that of Prime Minister Margaret Thatcher. Stephen Lewis, who looks desperately for his abducted daughter in the unforgiving cityscape, narcissistically projects his desire for her return onto the world around him, but learns through a series of dramatic confrontations to recognize others' individual needs, including his wife Julie's. His journey of discovery is facilitated by the text's unusual generic composition, which mixes the gritty realism of the city with magical passages in which time is experienced in alternative ways. Stephen's moral epiphany forms part of a fantasized resolution out in the woods, away from the problems of London, leaving the reader to question the ultimate meaning of his conversion for the contemporary world in the text.

Chapter 5, as I mentioned earlier, deals with two texts that take as their subject the lasting effects of Nazi totalitarianism. *The Innocent*, a blackly comic spy thriller set during the Cold War, uses a trio of characters—the English radio technician Leonard, his German lover Maria and her abusive ex-husband Otto—to act out the difficulties of escaping the grip of historical dominance and violence, which is symbolized by the egotistical masculinist attitudes and actions of both men. Jeremy in *Black Dogs*, in contrast, is a male character who innately recognizes the needs of others, a moral stance tested in an encounter with a father beating his young son, in which Jeremy must choose between his own welfare and that of the child. This historiographic text is set both in the recent past, around the time of the collapse of the Berlin Wall, and in the period just after the Second World War, when Jeremy's mother-in-law June was attacked by the black dogs who give the novel its title. The conflict between June's spiritual understanding of that event and her husband Bernard's rationalist denial of it forms the basis of the first-person memoir that Jeremy, a model figure of the ethical author, writes about them, which provides the generic frame for the novel. Both *The Innocent* and *Black Dogs* thematize the power of language and storytelling to reconcile historical and philosophical differences, though with widely divergent degrees of success.

The novel studied in Chapter 6, *Enduring Love*, opens with one of the most dramatic of McEwan's scenes of ethical decision making, as five men, including the narrator Joe, attempt to save a boy trapped in a drifting hot-air balloon. The choice faced by the men is a stark one, and the rightness of choosing altruism over egotism is parodically underscored by the actions of the erotomaniac Jed Parry, who refuses to acknowledge Joe's desire to be left alone. Yet the seemingly clear-cut moral issues in the text are complicated by its extreme degree of self-consciousness, with Joe as a highly unreliable first-person narrator overtly manipulating the construction of the narrative. *Enduring Love* has embedded within it multiple interpretive acts, such as Joe's frantic efforts to provide convincing evidence of Jed's harassment; this emphasis on interpretation as a difficult and unstable activity foregrounds the reader's engagement with the text as the crucial relationship between the self and the other in this case.

Chapter 7 groups together two short novels, *Amsterdam* and *On Chesil Beach*, written nearly ten years apart, that share tight dramatic structures leading up to climactic failures for its characters. *Amsterdam*, a satirical novel set during the waning days of neo-conservative government in England, centres on two male characters, the composer Clive Linley and his friend the tabloid newspaper editor Vernon Halliday, who embody the heartless self-interest of their society. Clive, the text's artist figure, is connected through intertextual references to the self-centred male poets of the Romantic period. In a scene clearly staged for the reader's reflection, Clive, when faced with the ethical dilemma of choosing between his art and a woman in trouble, makes the wrong choice. The ending in which Clive is punished for his arrogance along with his greedy and ambitious friend Vernon provides, as in *The Child in Time*, a comic resolution that does nothing to alleviate the oppressive political reality. *On Chesil Beach*, set in 1962 just before the dawn of the Swinging Sixties, is a period novel about a young newly married couple, Florence Ponting and Edward Mayhew, on their wedding night, unable to communicate to one another their anxieties about their imminent sexual encounter. Using the vantage point of a knowing contemporary narrator, McEwan frames the situation as a failure of narration and a series of unfortunate misreadings, with his characters' bodies as the texts under consideration.

In Chapter 8, I examine McEwan's most famous novel, *Atonement*, in which the question of ethics rests primarily with the text's author figure, Briony. As an adolescent, she falsely accuses Robbie Turner, a family friend and her sister's lover, of rape, and writes fiction as an act of atonement for that crime, which she committed because of an inflated belief in her own imaginative powers and a tendency to project her narcissistic desires onto others. The intricate structure of McEwan's novel, with its multiple sections and levels of narration, creates, I argue, a text so radically unstable in its representation that one is prompted to interpret Briony's authorial production not as penitential, but as a further sign of her narcissism. This highly self-conscious, deeply intertextual novel challenges the reader to think carefully about the relationship between fiction and morality.

McEwan's most topical novel, *Saturday*, set in London on the day of the massive protest against the imminent invasion of Iraq in 2003, is the focus of Chapter 9. The main ethical altercation in the text is the conflict between Henry, a surgeon with all the advantages of his society, and Baxter, an impoverished and mentally ill thug who menaces the doctor after a minor traffic accident. McEwan clearly establishes this relationship as analogous to the menace of international terrorism, with Henry's family home standing in for the threatened domestic nation. The highly focalized narration, which presents only Henry's point of view, subtly attempts to skew the reader in favour of the world view of that character, whose final defeat of his adversary is facilitated by the reading of a famous English poem. That self-conscious gesture, along with the novel's fantasy ending, which returns the middle-class family to its former privilege but represses the fate of those less fortunate, ideally should leverage a reading of the text as deeply ironic, which would obviate its otherwise troubling and imperialistic vision of contemporary British culture.

My 2005 interview with McEwan is followed by a chapter on his screenplays written during the hiatus period between 1981 and 1987, and collected in the two volumes *The Imitation Game and Other Plays* (1982)—which includes the television plays *Jack Flea's Birthday Celebration* and *Solid Geometry* as well as the title play—and *A Move Abroad* (1989), which includes the film screenplay *The Ploughman's Lunch* and the oratorio *Or Shall We Die?*. The chapter charts McEwan's efforts to write in dramatic forms, as he developed from his early experimental screenplays, which have subject matters and styles close to his short fiction, to the more conventional, but more accessible later works *The Imitation Game* and *The Ploughman's Lunch*, in which he represents political and personal power relationships in the Second World War and the early days of the Thatcher administration.

Collectively, these readings try to come to terms with the large and diverse body of work by a writer with a passion for human affairs and immense curiosity about the world, past and present. His oft-stated belief in fiction as a medium for improving our understanding and treatment of one another is reflected in his many representations of scenarios when characters grapple with moral choices, and are placed in the hands of his readers for ultimate judgement. At the same time, his increasingly complex aesthetic strategies put more demands on his readership to determine the real ethical implications of his texts, which sometimes are in danger of being lost behind the brilliance of his prose and the celebrity of his name.

2

A BIOGRAPHICAL READING

McEwan's biography, known to us from various interviews he has given and biographical pieces he has written, is in many respects an unremarkable one, and can only illuminate in part the wide array of characters, issues, historical contexts and aesthetic forms that he presents in his works. Certainly, McEwan's life story from his birth in 1948 to the present coincides with a period covering some of the major political and social changes in England and around the world over the past half century, and his intense interest in historical research, particularly into the Second World War and ensuing Cold War, broadens his available subject matter. In his recent book on McEwan, Dominic Head lists some of the key shifting cultural contexts that have bordered the author's life as "fading colonialism; the dissolution of the British class structure; educational reform; the transformation of family life; and the second wave of feminism" (5). As the following chapters will show, we can add to that list the rise and fall of British neo-Conservative politics and nationalism, the divisive effects of late capitalism, the threat of international terrorism and the creation of new models of masculinity.

Born in Aldershot, England, McEwan was raised in a military family by his father David, a Scotsman who was a sergeant major in the British army, and his mother Rose (née Moore) from the village of Ash, near Aldershot. Rose had been married before to Ernest Wort, with whom she had two children, Roy and Margy, McEwan's half brother and sister. Ernest died in 1944 after being wounded in the D-Day campaign. In 2002, McEwan learned that his mother and father had been having an affair before Ernest's death, and that they had produced an illegitimate child, who was secretly given up for adoption in 1942. This brother, also named David (Sharp), has made contact with his siblings, and has written a memoir about his life, *Complete Surrender* (2008), for which McEwan wrote the introduction, first published in *The Guardian* on Saturday, July 12, 2008 as "The child in time".

The decision to conceal David's birth was perhaps the result of the unequal relationship between McEwan's parents, a gender dynamic that seems to inform much of his fiction. McEwan describes his father as charming, gregarious, "handsome" and "domineering" (Hamilton 9), and recollects him as "a remote, organizing figure with a service revolver strapped around his waist" (*MA* 27). There were problems with drinking and spousal abuse, to which McEwan tried to put a stop once he was older, but his mother prevented him from interfering. Rose, on the other hand, McEwan recalls as "very gentle, very easily tyrannized" (Hamilton 9), yet he much preferred her company, and would hide from his father whenever possible. In a 2001 poignant article "Mother Tongue", written while his mother was quickly deteriorating with vascular dementia, McEwan claims that Rose, who was always tentative and shy about her less than refined speech, was the model for his early efforts at fiction:

> When I started writing in 1970, I may have dropped all or most of my mother's ways with words, but I still had her attitudes, her unsureness of touch. . . . I would sit without a pen in my hand, framing a sentence in my mind, often losing the beginning as I reached the end, and only when the thing was secure and complete would I set it down. (2)

There are shadows of both Rose and David in McEwan's fiction throughout his career—Stephen Lewis's parents in *The Child in Time*, who argue over whether or not to abort their child, with the father Douglas taking the dominant role over his wife Claire (though that novel was written many years before the revelation of McEwan's concealed brother); the older Lily Perowne and Briony Tallis in *Saturday* and *Atonement*, both of whom suffer from deteriorating memory loss; the many fathers, some cruel and some loving, who populate the pages of McEwan's texts.

For all intents and purposes an only child, his half-siblings having been sent away to live with other relatives, McEwan spent part of his childhood in Singapore and Libya, gaining from those experiences a vivid sense of the frightening reality of historical events such as the Suez Crisis in 1956, as he explains in the introduction to *The Ploughman's Lunch*: "For some weeks I lived in a tent with other children not so very far from a machine-gun nest" (27); but in an interview with Ian Hamilton he also described the bases he lived on as being "like small council estates anywhere in England. The sense of being somewhere foreign is down to things like sunshine and one or two servants" (10). He was separated from his family and sent to a state-run boarding school in Suffolk, Woolverstone Hall, when he was 12 in 1959, and he remembers weeping on the plane as it left Africa, but otherwise his school years were not traumatic; he was a mediocre student, and focused on not being a target for bullies, so he faded into the background: "Most people seemed to have a great deal of difficulty remembering my name. I was always being confused with some other kid who looked vaguely like me" (Hamilton 12). McEwan relates an incident when he chanced to see on the headmaster's desk a report with his name on it with the notations "Hopelessly shy," "Can't get a word out of him" and "An intimate boy" ('Mother' 3). Only when "the hormones started to flow" at age 16 or 17 did he become interested in making a mark, and started to produce good work under the tutelage of an English master who was "cynical and well read and a Leavisite" (Hamilton 12). He set his sights on studying and teaching English, and began reading contemporary English writers such as Iris Murdoch and William Golding.

After taking a year off, he attended the University of Sussex from 1967–70, reading English and French. Though he found the university "unexciting," "with no sparkle" (Hamilton 14), it was there that he first seriously thought of being a creative writer, producing plays for the stage, radio and television. He says that he started with no particular plan for the sort of work he would create: "The desire to be a writer really did precede the material" (Hamilton 15). He settled on fiction because he felt that it allowed for more "self-determination" (Hamilton 15), unlike poetry, which he feared would tempt him to imitate others' style too much. At the new University of East Anglia, where he went to pursue a Master's degree in 1970 and study under well-known writers Angus Wilson and Malcolm Bradbury, he gained exposure to contemporary American writers such as Norman Mailer, Henry Miller and Saul Bellow, whose work had a lasting influence on him. He also had the opportunity to write fiction as part of his dissertation, and those short stories became the basis of his first collection, *First Love, Last Rites* (1975), though he had already published some of the pieces with a good press before he left for a trip to Afghanistan with some friends in 1972. In the introduction to *The Imitation Game and Other Plays*, he describes that adventure as "a great liberation from a formal education that had seemed to have gone on too long," and recalls being happily introduced to "people who spoke of the world in specifically anti-rationalist terms" (12), including discussions of psychotropic drugs and mystical religions. He could never enter fully into that way of living, however, feeling "slightly separate from it" and more comfortable with the "intensely rational tradition" (Hamilton 16) into which he had been educated, including science, for which he has an abiding fascination. Once he returned from Afghanistan, he was "relieved . . . to have a room somewhere with silence and get on with some work" (Hamilton 17).

At the young age of 24, McEwan settled into a lifelong career as a prolific professional writer, producing new texts at an impressive pace that he maintains to this day. His domestic life has, it appears, been a source of both support for his work and turmoil: his first marriage to Penny Allen, a spiritualist whom he met at UEA, from 1982 to 97, was seemingly a happy one for some time, and he credits her with being "a rich of source of ideas" (Haffenden 173) about social and political issues. Yet when their marriage ended in divorce, McEwan had to deal with emotional distress and public notoriety when Allen, dissatisfied with the custody arrangements for their two sons, fled to France with one of the boys and refused to return. Allen and her new partner, Ismay Tremain (originally Steve Brown), pilloried McEwan in the press and made public demonstrations against the author. Eventually, they were ordered to pay a £1000 fine and McEwan regained custody. In 1997, McEwan married Annalena McAfee, editor of the *Guardian Review*'s literary supplement until 2006, and is a devoted father to his now-grown sons. It is difficult not to see similarities between his present comfortable lifestyle and that of his lead character, the neurosurgeon Henry Perowne in *Saturday*, who has a loving relationship with his successful wife Rosalind and his talented children Daisy and Theo. Indeed, the Perownes' beautiful townhouse bears a striking resemblance to McEwan's Fitzrovia residence, which he was gracious enough to let me visit for our interview.

Over the course of his career, McEwan has had consistent success in impressing reviewers and readers alike, and his fame has grown steadily to its current heights. Early recognition came in the form of the Somerset Maugham Award in 1976 for *First Love, Last Rites*, and then *The Child in Time* won both the Whitbread Novel Award in 1987 and the Prix Fémina Etranger in 1993. Despite being a well-known writer in England throughout the 1980s and 90s, his international reputation became secure with his winning of the prestigious Man Booker Prize in 1998 for *Amsterdam* after several previous nominations. *Atonement*, which became an international bestseller, garnered him several awards from 2002 to 2004, including the W.H. Smith Literary Award, the National Book Critics' Circle Fiction Award, the Los Angeles Times Prize for Fiction and the Santiago Prize for the European Novel. This novel was also the source of some controversy, as he was accused of plagiarizing the wartime memoir *No Time for Romance*, published in 1977 by Lucilla Andrews about her experiences as a nurse in a London hospital during the Second World War. McEwan, who lists Andrews's book in the acknowledgements in *Atonement*, denies that he did anything wrong; as was the case with an earlier allegation of plagiarism, in which it was claimed that he based his 1978 novel *The Cement Garden* on Julian Gloag's *Our Mother's House* (1963), McEwan has asserted that it is "almost impossible for a writer not to face accusations of copying at some point" (Hoyle 1). The popularity of *Atonement* set the stage for *Saturday* to enjoy similar success, which was enhanced by that novel's seemingly prescient anticipation of the terrorist bombings in London in July 2007, just after a few months after its release. *Saturday* was recognized with the James Tait Black Memorial Prize in 2006, and was followed by the short novel *On Chesil Beach*, which was named the Galaxy Book of the Year at the 2008 British Book Awards, where McEwan was also named Reader's Digest Author of the Year. He was awarded a CBE in 2000. (www.ianmcewan.com)

Regardless of the level of celebrity that writers achieve within the literary world, they rarely become household names until their work has been adapted for popular media. Several of McEwan's early texts have been adapted to film, including *The Cement Garden* (1984), screenplay by Andrew Birkin, who also directed *The Comfort of Strangers* (1991), screenplay by the well-known playwright Harold Pinter, directed by Paul Schrader; *First Love, Last Rites* (1998), screenplay by David Ryan, directed by Jesse Peretz; and *Butterflies*, from the short story, in 2005, screenplay and direction by Max Jacoby. As I mentioned in the Introduction, McEwan himself has written several screenplays for television and film; he also produced a respected version of Timothy Mo's novel *Soursweet* in 1988, and the screenplay for a critically unsuccessful but lucrative Hollywood movie, *The Good Son*, starring McCauley Culkin, in 1993. He also wrote the screenplay for the 1993 movie version of his novel *The Innocent*, directed by John Schlesinger, but he found the experience difficult: "Everyone—the director, the designers, actors, everyone—had their own ideas and came piling in. And you are suddenly knocked off your perch as the God in this machine. It is better to have someone take a free run at it" (Chotiner 1). Since that time he has been content to play different roles in the adaptation of his work to the big screen; he was Associate Producer for the 2004 film of *Enduring Love*, screenplay by Joe Penhall, directed by Roger Michell, which is discussed in detail in the final chapter of Peter Childs's *Ian McEwan's Enduring Love*, and Executive Producer for *Atonement*, screenplay by Christopher Hamilton, directed by Joe Wright, which won Oscars and Golden Globe Awards in 2008. When asked why he did not write the screenplay for his most famous book's translation into film, McEwan said, "I didn't want people sitting around a table—a producer, a director—telling me that I hadn't fully understood these characters" (Solomon 1). In an interview with Associated Press, he pronounced himself pleased with the final product, praising the director's "lush visual sense" and "real sense and eye for instinct, for the emotional heart;" he feels the film does its best to convey lead character Briony Tallis's thoughts without the benefit of internalized narration: "Even if you couldn't have access to her mind, you really got the sense of her mind just turning" (1). The director's technique of cutting back and forth between Briony's point of view and those of other characters simulates effectively the novel's complex narrative layers (see Chapter 6); and the film, with its artistic cinematography and dramatic appeal (not to mention its celebrity cast), has introduced McEwan to a new generation of movie-goers and readers.

Yet despite being in a position to rest on his writerly laurels for the remainder of his career, McEwan frequently disrupts his writing and domestic comfort to make efforts on behalf of causes that he believes are important. In our interview, when I asked him about his role as a public intellectual and the numerous demands it puts on his time, he confessed to having "mixed feelings" about it, and indicated that he receives daily requests to appear on television, make appearances, serve on panels, and so on; "The machine is always hungry," he said, ruefully acknowledging that "novelists, in one of the minor leagues of celebrity culture, can get drawn in to lend their voices to the babble" (see page 136). He clearly subscribes to the view that artists have an ethical obligation to act for the public good, and that the production of art, however morally enlightening, is not sufficient in and of itself to respond to the world's problems. His involvement in the feminist and anti-nuclear movements in the 1970s and 1980s laid the groundwork for a lifetime of activism.

One of the key ways that he has been participating recently in the public debate is by publishing articles, appearing for the most part in *The Guardian* originally, but then reprinted in major papers around the world. In 2005, for example, after he joined the Cape Farewell artists' expedition to the Arctic to learn more about climate change, he published "Save the boot room, save the Earth", a light-hearted piece about the parallels between the competition for the best outerwear in the ship's boot room and the international conflicts that contribute to the destruction of the planet. McEwan draws this conclusion:

> We must not be too hard on ourselves. If we were banished to another galaxy tomorrow, we would soon be fatally homesick for our brothers and sisters and all their flaws: somewhat co-operative, somewhat selfish, and very funny. But we will not rescue the earth from our own depredations until we understand ourselves a little more, even if we accept that we can never really change our natures. (2)

Despite having no scientific expertise, McEwan believes that it is important for him, along with other artists, to speak out on the urgent problems facing the environment, to address the moral failures, evident in microcosm of the boot room, that have brought the issue to a crisis point.

Recently, as well, McEwan has felt compelled to speak out on issues related to the rise of Islamism, which he says he "despise[s]," "because it wants to create a society that I detest, based on religious belief, on a text, on lack of freedom for women, intolerance towards homosexuality and so on" (Popham 1). In this case, he was coming to the defence of Amis, who had been accused of racism for his views about Muslims. But McEwan has written and spoken about Islam in other contexts, especially in his responses to the terrorist attacks in the United States on September 11, 2001. In an interview with PBS's Frontline producer Helen Whitney in April 2002 titled "Faith and Doubt at Ground Zero", McEwan, an atheist, is careful to explain that he does not attribute the evil of terrorism to religious faith in general or to Islam in particular:

> I don't believe there's any inherent darkness at the center of religion at all. I think religion is a morally neutral force. It's clearly deeply stitched into what we are. You find forms of supernatural belief in all cultures, Christian and Judaic visions of "sky gods" or whatever . . . But now and then, people rise up and perform terrible things in its name, just as people perform extraordinarily fine, courageous things in its name. (4)

With regard to the 9/11 bombers, he cites their lack of scepticism, their unquestioning belief that they will be rewarded in paradise for their actions, as the motivation for their willingnes to harm others: "People who feel they are on the path to a kind of eternal bliss are people to beware of" (4). He also charges them with "a failure of the imagination, of the moral imagination": "What those holy fools lacked, or clearly were able to deny themselves, was the ability to enter into the minds of the people they were being so cruel to" (2).

In an article dealing with the 9/11 tragedy, "Only Love and Then Oblivion", published in *The Guardian* on September 15, 2001, McEwan expresses a similar idea, but from a different perspective. This time, he turns his attention to the victims of the attacks: the "couple jumping into the void, hand in hand; a solitary figure falling with a strangely extended arm (was it an umbrella serving as a hopeful parachute?)"; the "San Fransciso husband" who "slept through his wife's call from the World Trade Centre" (1), and could only listen to her final message of love on his answering machine. With this piece, McEwan brings to life the people who suffered that day, helping his readers to the imaginative engagement with others that is "the nature of empathy, to think oneself into the minds of others" and that prompts us to ask the question "What if it was me?" (2).

This imaginative ability is crucial to McEwan's conception of morality, and it is integral to his understanding of the ethical role that fiction can play. In a 2004 interview, he stated,

> That sense that other people exist is the basis of our morality. You cannot be cruel to someone, I think, if you are fully aware of what it's like to be them. And to come back to a novel as a form, I think that's where it's supreme in giving us that sense of other minds. (Koval 2)

By recreating the victims of the Twin Towers as "characters" whose thoughts we can enter, however briefly, McEwan provides a compassionate connection with them that renders violence against them unthinkable. Similarly, McEwan allowed his readers to imagine the shock and bewilderment of Londoners in a piece he wrote for *The Guardian* on July 8, 2005, one day after the bombings of the city's transit system, called "How could we forget this was always going to happen?".

With his responses to both sets of terrorist attacks, McEwan posits imagination and compassion for others as the best means of countering and preventing violence. In these pieces, we find the intersection of the two ways in which Ian McEwan feels that he, as an artist, can play a role in creating a more morally attuned society: through his activism as a public intellectual, devoting his time to causes such as gender equality, nuclear disarmament and environmentalism; and through his fiction, which he views as a medium for enhancing people's compassionate abilities to imagine the lives of others. Of course, these two aspects of McEwan's moral agenda are intertwined; as we saw with his tale of the boot room on the Arctic ship, he uses storytelling to promote his activist aims, while he has also built into his texts characters who are writers and musicians, some more ethical than others, to serve as models of how he believes real world artists should—or should not—behave. In his own life, McEwan has striven to exemplify the principled artistic behaviour by acting publicly in response to the problems of the times in which he is living, and by writing fiction that challenges readers to reflect on their own ethical responsibilities.

PART II

Major Works

3

THE CEMENT GARDEN AND *THE COMFORT OF STRANGERS*

As early as 1980, V.S. Pritchett wrote in the *New York Review of Books* that McEwan's "subject matter is often squalid and sickening; his imagination has a painful preoccupation with the adolescent secrets of sexual aberration and fantasy" (31). Like the stories in his first two collections, his first two novels—*The Cement Garden* (1978) and *The Comfort of Strangers* (1981)—abound with scenes of incest, sexual abuse, sadomasochism, dismemberment and murder, yet their sensational aspects are complemented with a surprisingly mature style and thematic seriousness. The "moral dimension" (Head 46) of this early work has often been difficult for critics to discern behind the dead-pan narration and the apparent nonchalance with which gruesome details are reported. Yet, as Jack Slay, Jr. notes, the moral effect of these texts results from McEwan's "conscious desire to shock readers, forcing them to gaze directly into the horrors of contemporary society" (6). We come to see the incestuous, violent, twisted and psychopathic characters of McEwan's early work as "the embodiments of our neighbors, our acquaintances, ourselves" (7), products of a modern urbanized culture that breeds alienation, isolation, selfishness and exploitation of others. The arid London landscape of *The Cement Garden* offers no sense of the natural world or human community; like the father's garden, the city is hard and unyielding. The labyrinthine urban setting of *The Comfort of Strangers*, a modified Venice, acts as a projection of the disturbed state of mind of that novel's main characters, as they attempt to make sense out of the political and sexual power relations in which they find themselves.

Connected to the motif of oppressive urban life in these books is the act of domination: of adults over children, of children over each other, of men over women and women over men. In *The Bonds of Love*, Jessica Benjamin describes how domination warps the ethical relationship between the self and the other:

> Domination . . . is a twisting of the bonds of love. Domination does not repress the desire for recognition; rather, it enlists and transforms it . . . . . A vicious cycle begins: the more the other is subjugated, the less he is experienced as a human subject and the more distance or violence the self must deploy against him. (219–20)

In his early fiction especially, McEwan focuses on the destructive power of domination in intimate familial and romantic relationships, in which people are most vulnerable to coercion or abuse by others for their own selfish ends. In a 1987 interview, he commented, "I just have a habit of watchfulness. There are two areas where I look. One is how people are with their children, because that fascinates me a great deal. And the other thing is couples, married or otherwise" (Danziger 13c).

Children, and particularly adolescents—whom McEwan has described as existing on the "shadow line" between childhood and adulthood (Ricks 526)—are the sole characters in *The Cement Garden*; eventually left without parents, Jack, his older sister Julie and younger siblings Sue and Tom are exposed to their own desires and those of others. At the novel's beginning, the family is living "the humdrum life of the English lower-middle class" (Slay 38), complete with conventional gender roles. The repressive father, whose masculine behaviour Jack attempts to emulate, decides to pave over the garden, a natural space that he intends to subjugate to his will. When the father dies of a heart attack in the middle of the job, Jack smoothes over the impression of his face in the wet cement, erasing and thereby appropriating the inscription of his patriarchal power. The passive mother, confined shortly thereafter to her bedroom by illness, dies and the children collude to conceal her death from the authorities so that they will not be separated. They decide to hide the mother's body in the basement, encased in the remainder of the cement, from which her corpse later breaks free, just as she continues to haunt the children's guilty nightmares. As Gaston Bachelard points out in *The Poetics of Space*, the cellar is "the *dark entity* of the house, the one that partakes of subterranean forces. When we dream there, we are in harmony with the irrationality of the depths" (18). For Jack and Julie, the reality of the rotting corpse becomes more powerful than their daily lives: "When we were not actually down there looking at the trunk it was as if we were asleep" (141).

McEwan accentuates the enclosed psychic environment of the children's home before and after their parents' deaths by creating a situation of acute isolation. Jack describes how his family once lived "in a street full of houses," but "the other houses were knocked down for a motorway they had never built," leaving their home alone on "empty land," looking "a little like a castle, with thick walls, squat windows and crenellations .... [I]t looked like the face of someone concentrating, trying to remember" (28). The inhabitants of this self-absorbed fortress are seldom visited by people from the outside; they have no local relatives and even the children's friends are kept at a distance.

While the family home is figured as an enclosed environment that both conceals and reflects the power relationships of the society outside, the intense isolation creates a situation in which the children can try on sexual and social roles provisionally without the pressure to conform to accepted behaviours. Normally, the conventional gender roles of masculine dominance and feminine weakness symbolized by the father and mother in *The Cement Garden* would prepare the children to assume and perpetuate those roles based on their identification with the parent of the same sex. With no masculine model, Jack is able to abdicate his paternal role, preferring instead to sink into slovenliness and constant masturbation while entertaining fantasies about the intrepid yet fastidiously domestic Commander Hunt in the science fiction novel given to him by Sue. Although he harbours incestuous oedipal desires about Julie, who has taken over the maternal responsibilities, their sexual play is light-hearted and unanxious, and he is happiest when the guilt-ridden identification between Julie and his mother is broken, such as when he misrecognizes his sister on a bridge some time after their mother's death: "Great relief and recognition swept through me and I laughed out loud. It was not Mother of course, it was Julie, wearing a coat I had never seen before" (84). Sue, the most affected by her mother's death, retreats into a world of make-believe, while the youngest child, Tom, is content to dress up as a girl, so that he can imitate Julie in his games, and later to regress to infancy.

This safe world of role-playing is threatened only by incursions from the surrounding culture, which would seek to realign the children in conventional sexual terms. Julie's boyfriend, Derek, takes Jack out of the home into the macho world of the pool hall, where he feels powerless and humiliated. When Derek discovers Julie and Jack involved in sexual activity, he literally smashes apart their private world by demolishing the mother's cement coffin and calling in the authorities, symbolized by the "revolving blue light" (153) on the novel's final page. Yet despite the seeming moral degeneracy of the final scene, McEwan suggests that his two main characters have successfully negotiated their oedipal paths and are ready to assume caring and responsible adult roles. Now cleaned-up and well-dressed, Jack engages with Julie in "a long investigation of each other's bodies" (151), which is not so much a sexual act as a serious attempt to come to know one another as individuals. When Julie offers Jack her nipple to suck, the gesture is both maternal and passionate, bridging her roles as replacement mother and nascent sexual adult. The "infant" Tom, watching their lovemaking from his crib, is not traumatized as in the classic Freudian primal scene, but is lulled to sleep. McEwan says of this text, "I had an idea that in the nuclear family the kind of forces that are being suppressed—the oedipal incestuous forces—are also paradoxically the very forces which keep the family together" (Hamilton 21).

Conversely, in *The Comfort of Strangers*, McEwan shows how repressed desires, particularly those associated with traditional sexual dynamics, can lead to horrific acts of domination and self-destruction. English tourists Colin and Mary spend their vacation in a city that is like Venice (though never named as such), drifting in and out of sleep in their hotel room, recounting their dreams to one another, and wandering aimlessly through the streets, frequently at night. The city, with its twists and turns, becomes an extension of their explorations of each other and their own hidden fantasies.

They find their darkest desires embodied in the mysterious Robert, who encounters them in the street seemingly by accident, though he has been stalking them and taking pictures of them, particularly of Colin, for some time. Robert, who makes plain his hatred for feminists, uses sexual violence against his wife Caroline in order to shore up his phallic power, damaged by humiliations he suffered at the hands of his oppressive father and jealous sisters, and undermined by his inability to sire children. As Judith Seaboyer points out, Robert's "personal trauma" reinscribes "the trauma faced by patriarchal culture at the end of the twentieth century" (1999: 979) with the rise of feminism. Yet despite this "disruption of the 'dominant fiction' " (Seaboyer 1999: 979), as McEwan makes clear, the patriarchal world view persists.

One of the reasons for the durability of patriarchy enacted in *The Comfort of Strangers* is complicity, the willingness of both women and men to reproduce structures of dominance and participate in their own objectification. Benjamin argues that denying women's role in the perpetuation of male ascendancy is not only naïve but also detrimental:

> This has been a weakness of radical politics: to idealize the oppressed, as if their politics and culture were untouched by the system of domination, as if people did not participate in their own submission. To reduce domination to a simple relation of doer and done-to is to substitute moral outrage for analysis. Such a simplification, moreover, reproduces the structure of gender polarity under the guise of attacking it. (9–10)

In an interview, McEwan suggested that pleasure plays a part in people's willingness to dominate or be dominated by others: "there might be desires—masochism in women, sadism in men—which act out the oppression of women or patriarchal societies but have actually become related to sources of pleasure" (Haffenden 178). In *The Comfort of Strangers*, all three of Robert's "victims" entertain violent fantasies of their own, in which they brutalize or are brutalized by their lovers: Caroline is thrilled by her husband's violent beatings and murderous intentions towards her; "the terror and the pleasure were all one" (86–7), she tells Mary. Although Mary is mortified by Caroline's collaboration in her own victimization, she herself imagines "amputat[ing] Colin's arms and legs" and "us[ing] him exclusively for sex," a fantasy that is partially realized in Colin's dismemberment and murder by Robert and Caroline, a crime, the police tell Mary, that is "wearingly common" (98). Colin himself dreams of a machine that would immobilize Mary so that he could "fuck her, not just for hours or weeks, but for years . . . till she was dead and on even after that" (63). In all three cases, sex entails the complete degradation of one party by the other; this desire to dominate is manifested in conventional male/female terms regardless of the characters' actual sex, with the noticeably feminine Colin as the object of both Mary's aggressive lust and Robert's sadistic, homoerotic tendencies.

McEwan captures the reification of gender roles in the image of two dummies (anticipating Colin's stunted body at the novel's end) on a bed in a department store window. Like the often twin-like Mary and Colin, the dummies are "from the same mould" (11), yet one wears pyjamas while the other wears a nightie; they also have different accessories on their respective sides of the headboard: a "make-up cabinet" and a "nursery intercom" for the female versus the elaborate technological paraphernalia on the male side, "a telephone, a digital clock, light-switches and dimmers, a cassette recorder and radio, a small refrigerated drinks cabinet and, towards the centre, like eyes rounded in disbelief, two voltmeters" (11). The eye-like gaze from the male end of the console is just one of many images of scopophilia in the story (Seaboyer 1999: 963), while the "oval, rose-tinted mirror" (11) that hangs over and reflects the female mannequin marks her/it as the object of that gaze. The gendered binary in this scene is clearly embedded in the power structure of capitalism, with the male dummy holding a phallic pen with which he has supposedly just signed the cheque for the "huge sum" (11) required to buy the furniture.

Benjamin notes that this kind of persistent "gender polarity . . . creates a painful division within the self and between self and other; it constantly frustrates our efforts to recognize our-selves in the world and in each other" (172). McEwan captures this failure to recognize the other in *The Comfort of Strangers* through Mary's belated realization that the photo she is shown by Robert in his apartment is in fact a picture of Colin, and proof of Robert's dangerous intentions against them. This awareness comes to her first as "something . . . at the back of her mind, just beyond her reach . . . like a vivid dream that cannot be recalled" (65); when she tries to tell Colin what she has realized, he drifts off into sleep. The fact that the act of recognition is figured here like a repressed memory in a dream underscores the chronic inability of char-acters in this novel to see others distinctly, not as extensions of themselves; Colin and Mary, for instance, "often said they found it difficult to remember that the other was a separate person. When they looked at each other they looked into a misted mirror" (7).

The Comfort of Strangers contains many such moments when characters fail to see each other clearly. Caught up in their own desires and the gender and power relations of contemporary soci-ety, they turn others into fantasy objects and treat them violently or even destructively. In *The Cement Garden*, in contrast, there are occasional glimpses of real connections between people, as the orphaned adolescents—those "perfect outsiders" (Ricks 526), McEwan calls them—grow into the social and sexual roles of adulthood.

4

THE CHILD IN TIME

After a break from writing fiction in the mid-1980s during which McEwan concentrated on writing in other genres (see Chapter 11), he returned to the novel in 1987 with the critically success-ful *The Child in Time*. In this text, he draws on a more contem-porary political context, the right-wing government of British Prime Minister Margaret Thatcher (1979–1990), to create a textual world characterized by oppression of the poor, rampant com-mercial greed, political corruption and environmental degrada-tion. As Ben Knights points out, this text, set in a futuristic 1996 when Thatcherite policies such as state-licensed begging are so entrenched as to be taken for granted, is a "millenarian" novel with an "apocalyptic weight" (207–8) on its plot, which includes the looming possibility of nuclear devastation and catastrophic weather patterns. *The Child in Time* depicts a late twentieth-century London society in which any form of innocence seems to have been irrevocably lost, and morality and genuine communication have been replaced by heartless self-interest.

While *The Child in Time* has grittily realistic elements of social injustice, as Knights suggests, "it is as though the genre of real-ism is inadequate, as though the novel's project requires a shift of genre, or at least of narrative register, in order to accomplish its ends" (213). Evidence of this shift appears in various tempo-ral anomalies within the text's otherwise linear action, including the radical slowing of time during a motor vehicle accident—explainable perhaps, as Paul Edwards notes, as an example of Bergsonian "*durée*" (45)—and the movement into the past by the main character, Stephen Lewis, a scene later to be derided by

Henry Perowne in *Saturday* as part of that character's rejection of the magical realism of contemporary novels: "One visionary saw through a pub window his parents as they had been some weeks after his conception, discussing the possibility of aborting him" (67). These fantasy passages represent a melding of the infinite potentialities opened up by fiction (underscored by the many allusions to Jorge Luis Borges's "The Garden of Forking Paths" in the text) and the innovations of modern physics, articulated in the novel by Thelma Darke, a scientist who accepts as feasible ideas such as "backward flowing time" (45). This more flexible, "feminine" conception of the universe exists in tension in *The Child in Time* with the rigid, "masculine" world of the "real" London where Stephen, himself a writer, searches futilely for his daughter Kate, abducted in plain sight from a grocery store; his movement beyond the self-absorption generated by that loss to a state of altruism, visible in a series of key scenes of face-to-face encounter with others, is made possible by the text's generic double-life, though, I will argue, not in an entirely satisfactory way.

While *The Child in Time* uses its urban setting to convey the degradation of contemporary humanity, the city also contains within it the possibility of transcendence. This dual nature of McEwan's London corresponds with the two conceptions of urban existence described by Ihab Hassan in "Cities of Mind, Urban Words: The Dematerialization of Metropolis in Contemporary American Fiction". The real cities in which people struggle to live their daily lives are "intractable," he says; they

> lie athwart our will, astride our being . . . . Yet immanent in that gritty structure is another: invisible, imaginary, made of dream and desire, agent of all our transformations. It is that other city I want here to invoke, less city perhaps than inscape of mind, rendered in that supreme fiction we call language. (94)

Drawing on examples of idealized cities created over the centuries by Western writers such as Plato, Tommaso Campanella and Sir Thomas More, Hassan hypothesizes the existence of an ethereal urban realm that always subtends our lived experience. In its dematerialized form, "the city remains an alembic of human time, perhaps of human nature . . . . As a frame of choices and possibilities, the city enacts our sense of the future; not merely abstract, not mutable only, it fulfills time in utopic or dystopic images" (96).

With its interests in urban representation and alternative temporal realities, *The Child in Time*, plays these two conceptions of the city off one another. The "real" London cityscape in which Stephen Lewis searches for his daughter is blatantly dystopic: street-level violence is spontaneous and largely uncontrolled; nuclear rivals threaten universal destruction; sexuality is repressed or failing; and the innocence of childhood is about to be ruthlessly checked by the mandates of an official report. Remarking on London's decline, Stephen's father Douglas laments, "It's a new country. More like the Far East at its worst" (209); Stephen himself asks Thelma, "Everything's getting worse.... Isn't anything getting better?" (119). The material city, characterized by absolute loss, never yields up its missing child, and Stephen's marriage to Julie collapses under the strain. Between bouts of desperate searching, he spends most of his time alone, drinking and watching game shows that have condescending hosts and infantile audiences, anxious for recognition from the world of consumerism. He is involved in the work of the Child-Care Commission, ostensibly designed to help children, but the report for which, as Douglas rightly surmises, has been written in advance by ultra-conservative ideologues. The political world is typified by Stephen's friend the cabinet minister Charles Darke, a man with ambition but no convictions of his own, who is desired by the ambivalently gendered Prime Minister and is finally driven mad by the cynical and unethical practices of those in power.

Within this nightmarish urban world, however, Stephen gradually becomes aware of a parallel city that co-exists in the same spatial grid but is exempt from the constraints of temporal reality with its concomitant sense of loss. Stephen's access to this ulterior zone is apparently facilitated by a series of cataclysmic events—his daughter's disappearance, his consequent estrangement from his wife, a near-fatal car accident, Charles's suicide—that disrupt the rationalistic, "geometric" nature (19) of the real city and allow him to perceive time in unusual ways, such as being able to witness past events in the present. The narrator describes one of Stephen's epiphanic experiences of time as being like "walking alone into a great city on a newly discovered planet" (107). In this alternative urban reality, the emphasis is on recovery rather than loss: a lorry driver is miraculously saved from a wreck, and Stephen can intervene in the past to prevent his own abortion.

Language plays a crucial role in McEwan's competing visions of London, particularly the atemporal, creative one, which is closely associated with the writing of fiction. Within the dystopic landscape, the acquisition of language is viewed as dangerous, producing "a banishment from the Garden" (86) that should be delayed for children as long as possible. Words are used to constrain, as with the *Authorised Child-Care Handbook*, rather than liberate. For Stephen, however, as a successful children's novelist, "the written word is a part of the world into which you wish to dissolve the childlike self" (89); his view of language as opening up infinite "magical" (a key word in the novel) possibilities is clearly a self-referential gesture on McEwan's part, suggestive of fiction's potential to counterbalance the strictures of oppressive contemporary life. Language, too, provides a means of orientation, of mapping reality; Stephen worries that the preliterate Kate will not be able to read the notes he leaves for her, marking her way home.

In response to his desperation about Kate, his "invisible child," Stephen constructs a fantasy about her "continued existence" without which he would be "lost, time would stop" (2). Adam Mars-Jones reads Stephen's situation as "a narrative of pain and loss," but also as "a suppressed drama of symbolic ownership" in which the father's sense of bereavement is made to seem "artificially equal" (27, 28) to that of the mother. While the fairness of Mars-Jones's privileging of maternal feeling over paternal is questionable, it is true that Stephen's reactions to Kate's disappearance early in the novel are bound up with notions of possession; he thinks of her as "property" that has been "*stolen*" (15, italics in original), a metaphor reinforced by the supermarket setting of the abduction. Stephen's actions in response to the abduction are framed in conventionally masculine, aggressive terms: "He was going to find his daughter and murder her abductor. He had only to keep walking, remain attentive, and he would surely enter the force field that would warn him that she was nearby" (23). Julie, on the other hand, retreats to the country with her music and her books, turning inwards to confront her grief privately; this feminine "principle of selfhood, in which being surpassed doing" arouses "men's hostility" (60), claims the narrator through

Stephen's focalized perspective, entrenching him more deeply in his solitary and futile pursuit.

One sign of his narcissistic withdrawal into self is a failure to recognize others as individuals separate from his obsessive need to find his lost daughter. In this frame of mind, he sees all children, including the licensed beggar girl who approaches him on the novel's opening pages, as potential substitutes onto whom he can project his desire to have his daughter returned to him. When he mistakes a girl whom he sees out his car window for Kate and pursues her into her school, the scene unfolds as a double fantasy: the recovery of the girl herself and an opportunity for Stephen to regress into his own childhood, a recurrent desire that becomes more pronounced in his narcissistic state. So thoroughly does Stephen enjoy the experience that he almost seems to forget why he has leapt from his car on the way to an important meeting; it is as if he has stepped out of the normal course of temporality: "Time itself had a closed-down forbidden quality; he was experiencing the pleasurable transgression, the heightened significance that came with being out of school at the wrong moment" (166). This sense of illicit pleasure lasts while Stephen takes a seat in the schoolroom and takes part in a class exercise, drawing a medieval village with its tightly clustered huts and water-pump, a picture of traditional community, but he is confounded by the image of the manor house, a symbol of power separated from the other buildings, which forces him to "draw[ing] out of scale" (169).

Despite the timeless quality of Stephen's fantasized return to childhood, his experience in the school is marred by such images of separation and domination, reminders of the world he has momentarily left. Stephen feels he is in control of his transition back to adult life as he leaves the classroom: "These were moments of intense pleasure, the time it took Stephen to walk to the classroom door; to step out of the fantasy, to cease colluding in the teacher's authority . . . —this was his schoolboy daydream, nurtured through many dull hours, enacted at last, thirty years late" (171). Yet as soon as he has left the security of the class and resumes his search for "Kate" (actually another girl named Ruth Lyle), he becomes a strange man watching children, just like pedophile who presumably abducted his daughter, and is therefore subject to the punitive authority of the school.

The representatives of the school emanate masculine, repressive power; Stephen watches a male gym teacher giving instruction on the wooden horse, emitting "staccato . . . *hups*" that "never varied in tone" as "each child sprang to attention, military style" (168) after his or her turn. The headmaster whom Stephen is taken to see is similarly authoritative, "a lean military type" who "appear[s] to have been cut out of thick cardboard" (174). These figures recall the repressive political environment outside the school, with its menace of military action between nuclear rivals. The stern headmaster quickly dismisses Stephen's belief that the girl is Kate as wish-fulfillment, saying that he "must be wanting it to be her" (176). Recognizing the folly of his claims, Stephen shifts abruptly from unwavering certainty to a realization of how he has deluded himself: "Remembering how Ruth Lyle did and did not resemble his daughter, he understood how there were many paths Kate might have gone down, countless ways in which she might have changed. . . . He had been mad, now he felt purged" (179). This sudden return to the stark reality of Kate's probable death is foreshadowed by the skipping song that Stephen hears the girls singing outside the school; it begins, "*Daddy, Daddy, I feel sick, Send for the doctor, quick, quick, quick!*" (164), a call for paternal care; but the next verse continues, "*Doctor, doctor, shall I die? Yes my dear, and so shall I*" (165, italics in original), an expression of inevitable mortality. The unfillable void created by Kate's absence is further symbolized by the man who walks around the school grounds carrying an empty "zinc bucket" (179) for no apparent reason, just as Stephen wanders about London with his grief.

The ineluctability of loss even penetrates those scenes in which Stephen has access to the atemporal dimension of the city with its promise of miraculous recovery. For instance, during the sequence in which Stephen narrowly avoids a deadly car accident when a lorry suddenly loses a wheel and flips over in front of him, time is radically slowed, "duration shap[ing] itself around the intensity of the incident" (108). The event quickly takes on a mythical quality; the narrator notes, on Stephen's behalf, that "there was space too for a little touch of regret, genuine nostalgia for the old days of spectacle, back when a lorry used to catapult so impressively before the impassive witness" (107). Having saved himself through a feat of skillful driving, Stephen wishes he had had an audience of some sort, a passerby or a farmer in a nearby field, to admire and appreciate his proficiency; this note of theatricality and deliberate artificiality is common to the scenes of alternate temporality throughout the novel. Stephen's perception of the experience, focalized through the narrator, is that ordinary reality with its unforgiving physical laws has been suspended in favour of a new existence with more expansive possibilities; he imagines that there is "a sense of a fresh beginning," that "he had entered a much later period in which all the terms and conditions had changed" (107). The lorry driver, despite being crushed within the cab, is wondrously unhurt and emerges, "a bloody miracle" (113), with Stephen's help, head first from a "vertical gash" (109–10) in the steel. Knights interprets this image as a "hideous parody" (212) of the birth scene to come at the end of the novel, in which Stephen assists with the delivery of his second child and recalls with pleasure the memory "of a sunlit country road, of a wreckage and a head" (261). Stephen's heroic solo action of rescuing the lorry driver can also be seen as a fantasy of compensation for his feelings of helplessness around Kate's birth, when he felt that his "value had been more symbolic" (258) than actual, contributing to what Mars-Jones views as possibly "the crux of the novel: the male exclusion . . . from the reality of creation" (29).

Despite these miraculous acts of heroism, toasted lavishly by the lorry driver Joe with a bottle of champagne conveniently ready in the back seat of Stephen's car, there are small reminders of the real world that surface throughout this encounter with altered temporality. Once the lorry has finally crashed and Stephen can safely approach the wreck, elements of his everyday experience appear reframed and transformed. For example, the crushed cab of the truck first resembles "a tightly closed fist" (109), recalling his nasty run-in early in the novel with the beggar girl who wads his money into her hand then swears at him; it next resembles "a toothless mouth held shut" (109), suggesting Stephen's imaginings of Kate at the age of five losing her first baby tooth. Finally, the cab is compared to "a heavily furnished room" (109), the sort of domestic interior that Stephen lacks in his sparse existence after Kate's abduction and Julie's departure.

In fact, Stephen's inability to reunite with Julie and Kate undercuts the potential in this scene for recovery of that which seems to be irreparably lost. While he is experiencing the temporal distortion of the accident itself, Stephen imagines he is able to communicate telepathically with his wife and child:

> He beamed messages, or rather messages sprang from him, to Julie and Kate, nothing more distinct than pulses of alarm and love. There were others he should send to, he knew, but time was short, less than half a second, and fortunately they did not come to mind to confuse him. (107)

This fantasized act of communication is mirrored in Joe's dictation of messages before he knows that he will survive the accident. Stephen agrees to serve as amanuensis since "he was as amenable as any man to the necessity of final messages" (110). Joe's first message to his wife Jane expresses regret that he will not be able to return to domestic life with her and their children, a reunion he foresaw, he claims, in a dream the night before: "I was always going to come back. You know that, don't you" (111). Unlike Stephen's dedicated messages to Kate and Julie, however, Joe's first note is quickly succeeded by other, more self-serving messages: one to a male friend, giving instructions for the repayment of an outstanding debt (out of Jane's pocket, no less) and the care of a dog; and another to a former teacher, conveying resentment for that person's poor opinion of his prospects in life. When Joe begins a note to Wendy McGuire as "Sweetheart" (111), revealing his infidelity, Stephen immediately snaps his notebook shut and refuses to take any more dictation. After the rescue, Joe asserts that in repayment for his miraculous survival he is "going back to Jane and the kids and bugger Wendy McGuire" (115); yet that act of reconciliation is doubtful in light of Joe's general character and the fact that, in the contemporary world he inhabits, fidelity in marriage is dismissed as a "myth and cliché" (156). Stephen finds that he feels "encumbered" (115) by what is written in his notebook, contradictory messages about the kind of domestic life that he would cherish but can never have, so he "post[s] them all down a drain" (115) along with the postcard he had written to Julie seeking to renew contact with her, despite her desire to remain undisturbed.

Gradually, Stephen moves closer to recognizing that he cannot regain his lost relationships with his wife and child simply by wishing them into existence. Close to Kate's sixth birthday, he finds himself drawn to a nearby toyshop, contemplating buying her a present. He sees this as an act of "magical thinking" along the lines of other "small superstitions" (146) he has adopted to keep reality at bay: always shaving the left side of his face first, for example, or putting both feet on the floor simultaneously when he gets out of bed. He considers that the purchase will "be an act of faith in his daughter's continued existence" (146), a defiance of the almost certain fact of her death, likely by violent means. The narrator characterizes Stephen's action as a conscious effort on his part to reconceive his situation in different terms, closer to the transcendent reality he has glimpsed through his unusual experiences of time:

> Since he had exhausted all possibilities on the material plane by searching the streets, by placing ads in local papers and offering a generous reward . . . then it only made sense to deal on the level of the symbolic and the numinous, to conjoin with those unknowable forces that dealt in probability. (146–7)

Still, the narrator insists, Stephen has not lost his mind; he "kn[ows] what [is] real. He kn[ows] what he [is] doing, he kn[ows] she is gone" (148). There are constant reminders of the stark reality of the dystopic city: the toy store is laid out "in the style of a supermarket" (149), recalling the site of Kate's abduction; the toys for sale include pretend weapons, suggestive of the violence in London and the world beyond; the rain that had continued for "fifty days" (143) before finally stopping resumes, casting an apocalyptic pall over the scene.

Amidst this bleakness, Stephen attempts to construct a magical preserve; he gathers up items related to witchcraft and magic, and finds what he thinks is the perfect gift: a walkie-talkie set, with a picture on the box of a boy and girl "communicat[ing] delightfully across a small mountain range on what looked like the surface of the moon" (149). When he gets the set home, though, he discovers a label that reads "The maximum range of this device [. . .] is in accordance with government legislation" (149), a restriction reminiscent of the *Child-Care Handbook*'s many prohibitions. His magical ability to reach Kate curtailed, Stephen wraps the presents, only to find "a long nail smeared with fake blood in his hand" (150), which makes him suddenly aware of the falseness of the ritual in which he is engaged. The impossible task of covering over the dystopic reality is strikingly captured in the image of the wrapped-up toy witch's black cat, whose "tail protrude[s] from the paper and g[ives] itself away" (150). Finally, Stephen concedes the failure of his plan to conjure away his pain; the narrator relocates him in the world of temporality: "More than two years on and still stuck, still trapped in the dark, enfolded with his loss, shaped by it" (151).

Stephen's growing understanding that he cannot reshape reality in the image of his own desires coincides with his recognition that the fantasy of returning to a state of childish innocence, which he has harboured since the writing of his juvenile novel *Lemonade*, is only an illusion, like the story his father told him as a boy: "Stephen's father looked from the horizon to explain that trains got smaller and smaller as they moved away, and that to accommodate them the rails did the same" (54). While Stephen, as an adult, comes to accept the impossibility of such magical transformations, his friend Charles Darke provides an object lesson for him on the dangers of regressing into childlike tendencies. Darke, who resigns his pressure-filled Cabinet post, longs to experience the "timeless," "mystical" (238) aspects of youth that he never got to enjoy, so he hides in the woods and begins acting like a child, with his wife Thelma willingly playing a maternal role. He builds himself a tree house, which he joyfully proclaims as his "own place" (124), filled with boyhood paraphernalia. This retreat symbolically replaces Stephen's own unstable childhood homes; as the son of an RAF officer, he was frequently moved around and subject to his father's brutality, carefully concealed beneath military order. Darke himself, in effect, poses as a substitute for the novel's missing children in every respect, from Kate herself to the general loss of innocence.

Nonetheless, everything about Darke's retreat is pointedly exposed as grotesque and false. His adult head poking up through the hole in the tree house resembles, as Ellen Pifer suggests, "a kind of reverse birth . . . the most extreme and unnatural form of regression: an attempt to return to the womb" (203). The items in his pockets—a slingshot, marbles and so on—look to Stephen "as if his friend had combed libraries, diligently consulted the appropriate authorities to discover just what it was a certain kind of boy was likely to have in his pockets" (130); still, Darke constantly seeks Stephen's approval of the artifice that he has built. The only means of entering the tree house is by climbing a treacherous ladder of nails hammered into the trunk, foreshadowing the fake nail that Stephen will later buy at the toy store and that will snap him back to reality. Terrified of the ascent, Stephen is repeatedly warned by a laughing Charles that one wrong move will kill him; Stephen's survival through responsible self-care, in contrast with Darke's death later on, marks this scene as another "stage" in his "interior journey" (Pifer 201) away from childish narcissism.

McEwan stages Charles's self-indulgent imaginary return to childhood as a counterpoint to Stephen's own apparently literal regression through time early in the novel, made possible by the text's elastic representational mode. As Stephen begins walking from the train station on his way to visit Julie at her cottage in an attempt at reconciliation, he leaves behind the "sterilised domain of the novel's present time" (Knights 213), characterized by a "hypermarket" and a "geometrical forest" of commercially planted pines "uncomplicated by undergrowth or birdsong" (*CIT* 55), to enter the friendlier, more humane countryside, where donkeys "nod" and "purr" (55) and lorry drivers smile and wave to strangers. After this initial movement into a utopic pastoral past, Stephen's further movement out of his own time and space is facilitated by his trek across an "unbounded field of wheat," a "void" in which "all sense of progress, and therefore all sense of time, disappeared" (55). Edwards notes that, while this vast field likely represents in the text the sort of profitable "agri-business" promoted by right-wing governments, it is also an oceanic symbol that gives Stephen access to the "unbounded and eternal experience of the noumenal itself" (53), making possible an escape from his contemporary moment. Yet there is also the suggestion that the single-mindedness of Stephen's present life does not entirely disappear but rather becomes projected onto the environment: the field is described as "an obsessive landscape—it thought only about wheat," and does not evoke "any real sense of a destination" (56), recalling his self-absorbed wandering around London.

Once Stephen has traversed this liminal expanse, he is able to enter completely into the world of the past, which is ominously segregated from the present by "barbed-wire fences curving through the green gloom" (60). As Knights notes, this "time warp" (213) is accompanied by a spatial shift; the rigid line of pines transforms into a softer, more feminine "tumbling chaos" of "deciduous trees in full leaf" (*CIT* 62). Stephen seems at first to be in control of his shift into this ulterior zone: "He was in another time but he was not overwhelmed. He was a dreamer who knows his dream for what it is, and though fearful, lets it unfold out of curiosity" (63). Still, the scene has its frightening aspects for Stephen; the narrator describes him as "vulnerable . . . to what happened when he emerged from the plantation" (60), and his growing recognition that what he is experiencing is not a memory but something with "origins outside his own existence" (62) unsettles his normally egocentric worldview. Once he becomes aware that he has stepped into his parents' past at a point shortly after his own conception, and is watching their younger selves through the frame of a pub window as they come to terms with his mother's pregnancy with him, he is overcome with panic: "Quite suddenly, with the transforming rapidity of a catastrophe, everything was changed" (65). Unable to get his mother to acknowledge his gesture to her and thereby reaffirm his contemporary selfhood, Stephen is left with "a cold, infant despondency," "a bitter sense of exclusion and longing" (65), which leads to a complete devolution of his ego, back to a primordial, subhuman form with "scaly flippers" and "gills" (66). Metaphorically, through this movement into the past Stephen goes beyond Charles' "reverse birth" to a state of embryonic non-existence in which "nothing was his own" (66).

Stephen seemingly recovers from this diminished sense of self during his encounter with Julie immediately following the episode at the pub. Apparently having found him unconscious near the cottage and somehow moved him indoors, she "tuck[s] him" (68) into bed with a hot water bottle and tea, and is drawing him a bath, thereby providing the maternal care that Stephen's mother's lack of response had denied, precipitating his collapse. This scenario creates a less disorienting shift into the past, through recollection rather than temporal relocation, not only into Stephen's childhood, but also into his marriage with Julie and their time with Kate, whose presence remains inscribed in the bed in the form of "traces of pee from her early-morning visits" (67). The physicality of memory dominates this scene, with Stephen and Julie's intercourse as a return to security for him through re-entry into the vagina:

> Later, one word seemed to repeat itself as the long-lipped opening parted and closed around him, as he filled the known dip and curve and arrived at a deep, familiar place, a smooth, resonating word generated by slippery flesh on flesh, a warm, humming, softly consonated, roundly voweled word [. . .] *home*, home where he owned and was

owned. . . . Time was redeemed, time assumed purpose all over again
because it was the medium for the fulfillment of desire. (71)

In contrast to the terrifying devolution to pre-birth that Stephen
experiences, or at least imagines himself experiencing, outside the
pub, in this case the return to the womb is comforting, uniting
past and present, restabilizing language and restoring the sense of
"ownership" that has been lost to him since the abduction. Still,
Stephen considers the two events to be "undeniably bound, they
held in common the innocent longing they provoked, the desire
to belong" (70).

As the connection made between the pub and the cottage suggests, this scene is clearly focalized through Stephen's point of
view, and despite the apparent mutual nature of their lovemaking, McEwan inserts hints that Stephen's desire is dominant, as
well. His orgasm is symbolized by his hanging "in clear air . . . from
a mountain ledge" before falling "backwards into the exquisite,
dizzy emptiness" (72); hers is not mentioned at all, but she is
instead described as crying, though Stephen does not seem to
respond to that in any way. When they move beyond the physical and begin talking, immediately they are separate once more,
with Julie relating an "anecdote about life in the nearby village"
and Stephen giving "an exaggerated account of the committee
members" (72), reinforcing the urban/rural divide that defines
their relationship. At the same time, the oppressive environment of contemporary Britain reasserts itself, with "the plantation
trees . . . pressing in on all sides" (74), darkening the room, and the
"machine-efficient prairie" (73) lying just outside to facilitate his
journey back to the city. Julie's cottage, as he steps outside, looks
to him like "a house such as a child might draw" (74), anticipating
his abortive attempt to draw the medieval village in the school and
implying that his encounter with her has been yet another fantasized reunion constructed largely from his own self-centered perspective. The encounter ends with Stephen hurrying back towards
London to keep a dinner engagement with friends, leaving Julie
behind and then not seeing her for many months, expecting her
to "summon" (74) him without assuming any responsibility for
maintaining contact.

Stephen is able to see these interconnected events in a different light only after coming to terms with the importance of

acknowledging others' distinct experiences and needs. Towards the end of the novel, he seeks out his mother Claire's version of the conversation at the pub, inviting her to speak first before giving his own account; the shift in focalization throughout her narrative away from Stephen's perspective for the first and only time in the text underscores the increasing importance of imagining different points of view. Her story focuses on her realization, similar to June's in the scene with the dragonfly in *Black Dogs,* that the baby in her womb was "a separate individual . . . a life that she must defend with her own" (207), an epiphany brought about by her recognition of the boy outside the pub window as her own son. Despite this point of coincidence between the two stories, which redeems Stephen's wretched experience of apparent nonexistence, the two versions are not identical; once she has heard Stephen's side, she says, "It almost connects up" (209), suggesting there are subtle variations that only she knows. The partiality of her vision in his scene is captured in her wearing "a rakish eye patch" (194) after having lost "most of the sight in one eye" (193) due to illness.

Stephen's growing ability to recognize others as individuals beyond the scope of his own desire is also couched in visual terms. At the train station on his way to deal with Charles's death, he comes across the body of the homeless beggar girl from the opening scene of the novel, dead after considerable suffering, and looks at her clearly for the first time: "He tried to remember how he had seen Kate in this girl" (228). Thelma takes him to task for not having seen before—or heard for that matter—what was "right in front" (242) of him all the time: Julie, whose summons finally comes in the form of persistently ringing telephones.

By the time Stephen is finally reunited with Julie at the cottage, it seems that he has left behind his narcissistic tendencies and is fully able to see and embrace others on their own terms. Making his way from the train, he is conscious of his parents as individuals who made a difficult decision many years ago: "Where were those young people now? What separated them from him beyond the forty-three years?" (250). Having that new sense of historical connectedness, he can put his experience of temporal regression into perspective; the pub takes on the unreality that Julie's cottage had had, becoming "a bold pencil sketch" (251) in the winter light. Rather than focusing on the event at the pub as a measure of his own significance in the world, he imagines it instead as a stage in a process that will lead to new life for another: "It was then that he understood that his experience there had not only been reciprocal with his parents'; it had been a continuation, a kind of repetition. . . . All the sorrow, all the empty waiting, had been enclosed within meaningful time, within the richest unfolding conceivable" (251). The metaphysical continuum implied here is that Stephen's brush with non-existence through contact with his parents' "ghosts" prompted him to follow the "forking path" (70) that led to intercourse with Julie; his later receptiveness to his mother's version of the event moved him beyond self-absorption; and the logical outcome of this temporal "unfolding" is his return to the scene to reconcile with his wife and await the birth of his child.

Stephen and Julie's second encounter at the cottage is characterized by a noticeably different dynamic of communication, power and desire. At their last meeting, conversation had ruined their intimacy, as they had spoken disparagingly of others; this time, with their focus on their lost child, the coming baby, and their commitment to one another, they connect more deeply. The emphasis in their lovemaking here is on Julie's pleasure, which moves them beyond language as she cries out "something joyful he could not make out, lost as he was to meaning" (257). The bureaucratic power of official discourse as represented by the *Child-Care Handbook* is swept away, as Stephen is unable to find any "books on birth" (259), and instead must participate in the labour in a more natural way, working from memory and listening closely to Julie's needs. With no midwife present, Stephen's role in the birth is more than just symbolic; he actively assists in the delivery, but accepts without resentment the mother's greater importance to the newborn's well-being.

The birth of the child serves as the last of Stephen's experiences of altered temporality that facilitate his progression towards respect for the other. He feels "a slowing down as he enter[s] dream time," then is confronted with the physical presence of a new being demanding recognition: *"Had you forgotten me? Did you not realize it was me all along? I am here. I am not alive"* (261, italics in original). This question "from life itself" (261) unites the missing child Kate with all children, redeeming for Stephen and Julie the inhumanity of "the government, the country, the planet" (256), the "harsh world" (263) symbolized by the appearance of Mars in the sky and the sound of the midwife's feet coming up the path. Julie and Stephen begin to establish the baby's sex only in "acknowledgement of the world they were about to rejoin" (263), suggesting that the gender differences that divided them in the city do not exist in the bucolic environment of the cottage.

Yet this idyllic ending, the culmination of the novel's fantasy passages, implies that such harmonious understanding is possible only in the country, away from the harsh conditions of the intractable city. Despite Stephen's dawning appreciation of others' needs, there is nothing to suggest that the heartless world of neo-conservative London has changed at all; in fact, the release of the *Child-Care Handbook* shortly before Stephen's final trip to the cottage has ushered in a new era of "common sense" (214) that promises to be even colder and less compassionate. There are signs, too, that the negative effects of contemporary urban capitalism are beginning to encroach on the redemptive world of the countryside. Stephen's journey to get to Julie begins with his return from the woods where the Darkes have their retreat to London, where he must get to Victoria Station to catch his train. The "nearby soup kitchens" (245) are reminders of the city's brutal poverty, and the taxi driver whom Stephen engages is almost tempted by the offer of £2,500 to drive all the way to Kent. Edward, the engineer of the maintenance train who allows Stephen to ride in the cab, thereby fulfilling his "boyhood dream" (253), demonstrates the opposite of urban greed by declining Stephen's offer of payment, having quickly guessed that Julie is about to give birth and will need the money. This model of rural community life is disrupted, though, by the government's plan to sell off the land around an old railway tunnel at the end of his line, a beautiful "cathedral in the dark" (249) to be destroyed for the purpose of building yet one more motorway.

Eventually, then, the rural paradise that is the text's site of magical renewal will be overrun by the degradation and inhumanity of the city, leaving the reader to wonder at the viability of Stephen's ethical awakening. By tying the gradual process of coming to see others on their own terms to scenes of otherworldly experience, McEwan insists on a divide between a fantasized moral life and a ruthless contemporary reality, without offering any means of reconciling them. The dream city of compassionate human interaction remains an elusive fiction in *The Child in Time*.

5

THE INNOCENT AND *BLACK DOGS*

While *The Child in Time* confronts the moral failings of contemporary Britain, McEwan's next two novels, *The Innocent* (1990) and *Black Dogs* (1992) engage with the large-scale social and historical effects in the aftermath of military conflict in Europe during the Second World War. The first of these two more historically oriented novels, *The Innocent*, set in Berlin during the reconstruction of that city in the 1950s, is a Cold War spy thriller in which the lingering violence of the Nazi era is exacerbated by Germany's post-war political masters, the British and the Americans, with both groups imposing their imperialistic power. *Black Dogs*, though partly set in the present, is largely retrospective, exploring the collapse of that power with the fall of the Berlin Wall in 1989, but also recalling the ruthless repression by the Gestapo in France during the War. In both these texts, the domination of the state apparatus over its citizens, whether historical or actual, mirrors the unequal, and often detrimental, power of one person over another.

As I suggested in the Introduction, the writings of philosopher Emmanuel Lévinas provide a valuable framework for understanding the connection between personal ethical behaviour and state oppression in *The Innocent* and *Black Dogs*. Citing Lévinas's ideas, Tim Woods calls the fundamental principle of totalitarianism the "absolute denial of the other as Other" (54). When one person does not recognize the separateness of the other, violence and despotism are the result: "What characterizes violent action, what characterizes tyranny [...] is that one does not see the face in the other" (*Collected Philosophical Papers* 19). For human relationships to be "founded not on violence but on love" (Woods 55), Lévinas asserts, people must acknowledge others in the world in their distinct being, recognize their irreducible difference from us.

These novels reveal a new interest on McEwan's part in exploring the difficulties of creating and maintaining the kind of ideal relationship described by Lévinas, an effort intricately connected to the power of language. In each of these texts, the characters attempt to understand themselves and others by telling stories to one another, stories about their pasts or about things that have just occurred. At times, their efforts at communication are frustrated by manipulation of language in the form of propaganda or state secrecy, as in *The Innocent*; at other times, as in *Black Dogs*, characters have difficulty in interpreting or believing the stories of others owing to the unreliability of memory or the tendency for historical events to become transmuted into personal mythologies. Often, characters fail to communicate with each other at all, keeping their thoughts and feelings hidden, with the reader being privy to the various points of view only through McEwan's extensive use of focalized narration. This kind of failure is particularly acute in the relationships between male and female characters; as Maria Eckdorf, the German lover of English technician Leonard Marnham in *The Innocent*, puts it, "men and women don't ever really get to understand each other" (266). While narrative plays a central role in reconciling conflicting perspectives and individuals in *Black Dogs*, the related forces of historical oppression and masculine dominance combine to defeat the ethical potential of fiction in *The Innocent*, at least within the world of the text.

The Cold War setting of *The Innocent* lends itself to a focus on language as a medium of political control, with propaganda rife and truth measured out in official categories. Bob Glass, Leonard Marnham's American contact in Berlin, tells him that "everybody thinks his clearance is the highest there is, everyone thinks he has the final story" (16), but there is always another level of understanding just out of reach. In fact, argues Glass, the impetus to "invent language" (43), the basis of human culture, came from the understanding that one can choose to share or conceal information: "Secrecy made us possible" (44). Secrecy is fundamental to the novel's historical context, which is based on the actual joint American–British construction of a covert tunnel in Berlin in 1955 for the purpose of intercepting and decoding Russian messages. But the withholding and sharing of information is also central to the text's romantic plot, in which Leonard and Maria attempt to understand one another across the lines of gender, culture and experience that divide them.

Leonard and Maria first meet because of an act of communication that she initiates: she sends a message via a pneumatic tube system in a West Berlin nightclub to "the young man with the flower in his hair" (44). Leonard, who had tucked a rose behind his ear as a joke to his American co-workers Glass and Russell, is thus immediately established as the more passive of the two, and even somewhat effeminate. While Maria demonstrates Russell's belief that "Berlin girls were the liveliest and most strong-minded in all the world" (39), Leonard cannot emulate the confident, manly behaviour of the Americans around him, but rather reveals himself to be a shy, nervous Englishman, whose sheltered life has left him innocent about the world, and virginal. Maria, with her excellent English skills, five years seniority and sexual experience, has the advantage in the relationship, and she feels that Leonard's virginity liberates them to move beyond conventional gender roles of male dominance and female seduction to "invent their own terms" (65). She believes herself to be safe from the kind of sexual abuse that she suffered during the war and at the hands of her violent ex-husband, Otto. In her tiny apartment, she and Leonard retreat to perform his sexual initiation and to share stories of their pasts. When Leonard tries to "recount in an amusing way a sermon he had once heard at school about the devil and temptation and a woman's body" (69), he realizes that he has offended her, and she readily accepts his apology and forgives him.

This easy communion does not last, however; as Leonard gains confidence in the relationship; he is no longer comfortable with his role as Maria's tractable sexual student. Angela Roger points out that, by approaching Leonard in the bar and taking the lead in their first sexual encounter, Maria "usurps the traditional role of the man's sexual superiority" (24). As he asserts a more conventional masculine authority, his attitude begins to reflect the imperialistic dominance that Britain was striving to regain over Germany after the war.

Throughout the novel, McEwan draws the reader's attention to parallels between Leonard and Maria's romantic relationship and the Cold War environment, with the tunnel, as David James notes, presented as a "trope [that] performs a straddling act, serving textual and political duties" (91). Maria's bed, for instance, is described as the site of various "excavations" (*TI* 88) as Leonard explores her body; the bundles of wires in the tunnel are "held in bunches like a little girl's hair with a bright new clip" (189), recalling the "childish clips" (54) that Maria usually wears. Connections between the personal and the political are also perceptible to the characters themselves. While Glass regards Maria and Leonard's engagement as a model of "Anglo-German cooperation," she rejects that allegorical interpretation, asking Leonard, "Does he think I'm the Third Reich? Is that what he thinks you are marrying? Does he really think that people represent countries?" (158). Leonard, on the other hand, is attracted to the idea of replacing individual with political identity; his impression of Maria is that she has "the sort of face, the sort of manner, onto which men were likely to project their own requirements" (54). He starts to imagine her as "defeated, conquered, his by right" (94), a captured German woman whom he is entitled to rape as a victorious British soldier at the end of the war. When he attempts to act out this fantasy and she recoils in horror, he likens the situation in his mind to a childhood memory of a toy train that he over-wound, while she remembers witnessing as a child the rape of an injured woman by a Russian soldier. The startling incongruity between these two memories points to Leonard's utter inability to understand the horrific associations of his fantasy for Maria, and his failure to see her as more than an mechanical object for his amusement; he even imagines drawing "an emotional circuit diagram for her" (112) that would chart her inevitable forgiveness of him.

While Leonard is unable to recognize Maria's experience of the world and emotional needs as separate from his, she does manage to forgive him and resume their relationship because she is capable of imagining the reasons for his actions. Even when Leonard traumatizes Maria again by abruptly reaching out to touch her in the dark outside his apartment—the dark, like his myopia, symbolizing his general inability to see others clearly—she understands that he means her no real harm: "She had come slowly to the decision that Leonard was not malicious or brutal, and that it was an innocent stupidity that had made him behave the way he had" (124). We learn about Maria's insight from a third-person narrative voice that shifts in this scene back and forth from her perspective to his, giving us access to each character's unspoken thoughts and creating a sense of potential reconciliation between the two sides, at least in the reader's mind. After revealing Maria's conclusion that she can forgive Leonard, the narrator provides a sympathetic glimpse into his thinking: "To get up close in the dark and hold her hand, that was all he had wanted, to illuminate the old terms with touch" (125). When Leonard finally does express his remorse and his love to Maria, she is "fascinated, the way she had been once as a girl when her father had removed the back of a wireless set and shown her the bulbs and the sliding metal plates responsible for human voices" (126). Unlike Leonard's idea of the "emotional circuit diagram," which suggests that he can presume to map out Maria's responses without her articulating them, this mechanical image involves an act of imaginative engagement, a sense of listening in wonderment for the source of other "human voices."

Maria's empathetic treatment of Leonard leads to their reconciliation, and prompts him to be more imaginatively engaged with others. Otto's assault on Maria helps him realize that "he knew nothing about people, what they could do, how they could do it" (137), and causes him to feel genuine shame for his own violence. He consoles Maria by speaking in German, illustrating a new desire to bridge the cultural divide rather than being an imperialist master. Yet despite all this progress towards greater recognition of the other, Maria and Leonard as a couple never recover their original closeness and have to content themselves with "blissful ordinariness" (134). The reason for this decline in their relationship lies in the lasting effect of past violence, an influence that persists in both the personal and the political dimensions of the novel. Maria blames Leonard's "naughtiness" (133)—a word resonant of his childlike "innocent stupidity"—for their slide into conventional gender roles; it seems that Leonard's assertion of masculine dominance has ruined forever their ability to "invent" their own terms for their union, which would include some element of female ascendancy.

Maria's history with oppressive male power surfaces literally in their bedroom in the form of Otto, whose palindromic name suggests that going forward and going backward are the same. Although Leonard tries to imagine himself in advance of this encounter as a Hollywood "peaceable tough guy, hard to provoke, but once unleashed, demonically violent" (144), he knows he is no match for Otto's brute strength, and comes out of their fight with badly injured genitals, a sign of his final emasculation in the text, which correlates with Britain's reduced status in the world after the war. Much of Otto's power in this situation derives from his questionable reputation as a Nazi war hero, which makes him immune from arrest and leaves Maria and Leonard with no recourse but to deal with him themselves. Like the overthrown violent regime he represents, he has his identity effaced, starting with Leonard's biting off a piece of his cheek. As Rudolf Bernet argues in "The Encounter with the Stranger: Two Interpretations of the Vulnerability of the Skin", the infliction of "artificial or forced openings called 'wounds'" (Bloechl 45) signifies the penetration of the border separating one individual from another, the absolute denial of otherness. Otto's injury and subsequent murder and dismemberment mirror the carving up of Berlin into zones by the Russians and the Allies after the war; Leonard even imagines the corpse as "a city far below that [he] had been ordered to destroy" (200–1). As was the case with the Allies' defeat of the Nazis, this total obliteration seems justified—"We did what we had to," Maria declares (252)—yet the ongoing effects of that violent act, like those of Leonard's near-rape, are hard to escape. Leonard's blackly comic journey around the city trying to get rid of the bags of body-parts, a scenario reminiscent of the grotesqueries of McEwan's earlier work, serves as a parody of post-war German remorse: "Berlin was full of people with heavy luggage" (208). In his nightmare of reassembling Otto's body, Leonard experiences the guilt, too, of the Allies who destroyed so much of civilian Germany; on his arrival in Berlin, he is proud of the damage inflicted on the enemy, but then comes to see his pride as "puerile, repellant" (56) and marvels at the resiliency of the German people in their work of reconstruction.

The lingering effects of his violence render Leonard incapable of stabilizing his own situation in Berlin. While he manages to dispose of the bags in the tunnel, oddly enough by telling Glass, who does not believe him, honestly what is in them, he loses faith in the power of the truth and refuses to tell his story to the officials, though he repeats it obsessively in his mind: "He recounted his version, it was all he ever did . . . . There were no truths waiting to be discovered. There was only what could be imperfectly established by officials who had many other things to do and who would only be too pleased to be able to fit a crime to a perpetrator, process the matter and move on" (242). Maria, on the other hand, still believes in the power of language to persuade another of the truth of her situation; in her letter to Leonard years later, she explains how she broke the code of secrecy and confided in Glass: "Because he was being so kind and concerned, I broke down and cried. And then before I knew it, I was telling him the whole story" (263). This confession saves both Leonard and her from prosecution, as Glass arranges for the crime to be hushed up, but makes Maria swear not to tell Leonard. Her decision to maintain secrecy leaves Leonard unaware of his safety from the police and thus unable to live comfortably in Berlin, effectively setting the stage for his return to England without her. Preparing to leave the country, Leonard feels a common bond with the politically voiceless East German refugees he sees at the airport: "What all these passengers had in common was their innocence. He was innocent too, but it would take some explaining" (250).

In her 1987 letter to Leonard, which apparently prompts his visit to Berlin the same year, Maria nostalgically recalls his innocent ways but also berates him for being "so English! so male!" (267) that he did not speak up to challenge Maria and Glass regarding his suspicions about them. Her choice to marry Glass signals the triumph of American openness, manifested in the casual dress and sports-playing of the US tunnel-workers as well as the omnipresent pop music, over the British reserve and elitism represented by Leonard throughout the text. Maria's transformation mirrors that of Berlin itself, which, the older Leonard observes, has become Americanized, with "Burger King," "Unisex Jeans" and "McDonald's" (256) signs visible in the cityscape. Further, Glass's emotional responsiveness as a father serves as a contrast to Leonard's traditional conception of masculinity as tough and domineering. It is telling that the novel concludes with Maria having taken the step to initiate communication, just as she did at the story's beginning, whereas Leonard's only response is to wander Berlin alone, imagining their return to the city together.

While *Black Dogs* is also set partially in Berlin and, like *The Innocent*, has the aftermath of the Second World War as its historical backdrop, it presents a far more positive vision of the potential for human beings to overcome their violent tendencies and form truly caring relationships. The central political event in the text, the fall of the Berlin Wall in 1989, is anticipated by Leonard's 1987 wish at the end of *The Innocent* that he and Maria would one day "take a good long look at the Wall together, before it was all torn down" (270). The reconciliation of East and West Germany, described by the narrator Jeremy as the "marrying" of "two systems" (*BD* 50), takes place in parallel with the movement towards understanding between individuals separated by deep personal and philosophical differences.

As in *The Innocent*, the political allegory centers on a male/female romantic union, in this case the marriage of Bernard and June Tremaine, who, like the East and the West, seem to occupy diametrically opposed positions, aligned in their case with conventional gendered conceptions of men as more inclined towards rationalism than women; Jeremy describes Bernard and June respectively as "rationalist and mystic, commissar and yogi, joiner and abstainer, scientist and intuitionist . . . the extremities, the twin poles along whose slippery axis [his] own unbelief slithers and never comes to rest" (xxi). Jeremy's in-laws, having met towards the end of the Second World War and sharing an idealistic support of Communism, began their relationship with a sense of common values and romantic passion, but gradually became estranged from one another owing to profound disparities in their ways of seeing the world. Bernard recounts an incident from early in his marriage when he and June had come across a particularly beautiful dragonfly, which he, as a scientist, wished to kill and preserve. In her emotional response to the incident, June chides Bernard for being "cold, theoretical, arrogant" (54), an attitude he extends, she feels, towards the working-class people he claims to want to help through his political affiliations. To her, the insect represents all vulnerable beings, including the child in her womb, and Bernard's action was bound to lead to "something terrible" (56) happening to their baby; she feels vindicated in her belief when Jenny, who would later be Jeremy's wife, is born with a sixth finger. To Bernard, this sort of "magical thinking", which he finds "completely alien" (57), is symptomatic of the unbridgeable divide between men and women.

The differences in gender and worldview at the heart of June and Bernard's relationship also characterize the defining event of the novel: June's encounter with two enormous black dogs left behind by the Gestapo, one male and one female, while hiking with Bernard near the Gorge du Vis in France a week or so after the incident with the dragonfly. With Bernard lagging behind to study some caterpillars, June confronts the dogs alone, realizing in the process that she has "physical courage" of her own, "a significant discovery for a woman" (35) at that time. This recognition of her own strength is a sign of Bernard's diminishing masculine power over her, reinforced by June's complaints in later life about his "small penis size" (10). In the hiking scene, the shift towards greater female power is evident in June's decision to attack the male dog, the more aggressive of the two, using a phallic weapon—a penknife. With her successful repulsion of the dogs, June gains not only physical but also spiritual power; she is henceforth convinced of her own belief that the animals were symbols of a higher reality, that they "emanated meaning" (120), over Bernard's rationalist arguments to the contrary.

For June, this event becomes the turning point in her life, leading to a religious awakening and her eventual break with Bernard. With frequent retellings, the biographical fact of the encounter with the dogs, as Jeremy notes, has evolved into "a myth, all the more powerful for being upheld as documentary" (27). As Ernst Cassirer argues in the second volume of his *Philosophy of Symbolic Forms: Mythical Thought*, "what distinguishes historical time from mythical time is that for mythical time there is an absolute past, which neither requires nor is susceptible of any further explanation" (106). For June, this particular story——unchangeable, infinitely repeatable and undeniably mystical in significance—— acts as an insuperable barrier to her having a close relationship with Bernard, who could never consider the incident from her point of view. Even though they continue to love one another, a "shadow" (19) exists between them, so that they "couldn't make a life" (29). Rather, they live apart, telling Jeremy competing and contradictory accounts of their past, shaped by their individual memories into sacrosanct personal myths. These stories, such as their differing recollections of their first sexual encounter, lead to mutual accusations of "cooking the books," as Bernard puts it, prompting Jeremy to urge them to "put the record straight" (63) by talking to one another. Unable to bring themselves to do so, June and Bernard speak through Jeremy to each other, becoming debating yet disconnected voices in his mind that he attempts to understand and reconcile.

Jeremy's decision to achieve this act of imaginative reconciliation through writing establishes him as a model of the sort of author favoured by McEwan, a figure who moves towards a position of greater understanding of the other through compassionate curiosity, and feels compelled to express his insight through storytelling. Jeremy speaks openly about his decision to produce a textual record—"not a biography, not even a memoir really, more a divagation" (15)—of his relationship with his in-laws, and keeps his focus squarely on his subjects at all times. He devotes considerable energy attempting to perceive June's true face behind the photographic images of her early in her marriage, and, in a scene anticipatory of *On Chesil Beach*, he tries to comprehend the enormous pressures and confusions surrounding sexuality when they were young. Despite his presence as first-person narrator, Jeremy spends very little time on himself or even on his own wife and children in the memoir.

The one personal element he allows himself is a revelation of his own ethical transformation, which he seeks to communicate through the medium of his text. Addressing his readers directly in the form of a preface, Jeremy explains how his parents' deaths and his exposure to domestic violence with his older sister Jean and her lover Harper had left him with "blackness, the hollow feeling of unbelonging" (xii). This image of spiritual darkness, related to the blackness of the evil dogs as well as to a frightening dark shape Jeremy sees at his family's summer home, is eventually replaced for him by what June calls "the healing power of love" (37), While Jeremy has difficulty in accepting this concept in religious terms, what does fill his "emotional void" (xx) are his personal relationships—with various substitute parents, especially Bernard and June; with his traumatized niece Sally; with his own wife and children, who remain in the background of the text as figures of loving stability. In this respect, Jeremy represents a different model of masculinity than the often self-centered, aggressive male characters in McEwan's earlier work; his focus is always on the well-being of those around him, as is evident in his caring and responsible actions towards his family. As he gradually recognizes the power of this altruistic stance, which in return gives him the sense of belonging he had long craved, he loses his fear, heightened by his many conversations with the spiritualist June and the rationalist Bernard, that he has "no good cause, no enduring principle, no fundamental idea with which [he] could identify" (xx); instead, he becomes persuaded of "the possibility of love transforming and redeeming a life" (xxii).

This realization, founded on the compassionate recognition of the other, is central to the novel's response to violence and the enduring effects of totalitarianism. While June's encounter with the Gestapo dogs is ultimately a redemptive experience, the malicious stories of a young French woman raped by the animals during the war continue to incite angry confrontations many years later when Jeremy makes inquiries in St. Maurice, the village near the site of June's attack. Jeremy's recollection of his visit with Jenny to a Nazi concentration camp in Poland in 1981 brings to his mind not only the ongoing denial of Jewish suffering but also the ease with which anyone could slip into the role of the oppressor: "This was our inevitable shame, our share in the misery. We were on the other side, we walked here freely like the commandant once did" (88).

The fall of the Berlin Wall, a potent sign that the hostility of the post-war years was finally abating, is itself the occasion for an act of brutal suppression in the novel, in which a group of skinheads nearly beats a young communist to death. In this scene, however, the power of altruism triumphs over self-preservation. In an uncharacteristic gesture towards the irrational, Bernard indulges the fantasy after June's death that, at times, she is trying to communicate with him by appearing in the faces of others. When two young women pass him and Jeremy on their way to the Wall, Bernard is certain for a moment that one of them has "June's mouth and something of her cheekbones," and is therefore a "message" (61) to him from his wife. Yet when Bernard tries to defend the young communist, who reminds him of his own misguided belief in the Communist dream, and is saved by the same young woman, the rationalist in him refuses to accept Jeremy's view that she is actually "his guardian angel, the incarnation of June" (76). Bernard's temporary treatment of the young woman as the image of his own desire gives way to his willingness to put himself in mortal danger to protect a total stranger. Witnessing this benevolent act becomes part of Jeremy's ethical transformation, giving him the courage to sacrifice himself on behalf of the less powerful, even "to the point of dying for the other."

In a scene that parallels Bernard's confrontation with the skin-heads, Jeremy acts to save a boy being brutalized in a Paris restaurant by his parents, especially by his father, reviving the images of masculine aggression and child abuse associated with Jeremy's own childhood. Although he recognizes his own suffering as an orphan in the boy's plight, his identification is not self-serving but rather moral. When he challenges the boy's father and mistakenly says in French, "Are you frightened of fighting someone your own size, because I would love to smash my jaw" (107), he figuratively takes the boy's punishment onto himself. As his violent impulses overcome his urge simply to help the boy, however, Jeremy has to be prevented from "stomp[ing]" the father "to death" (108), just as the skinheads planned to do to Bernard. The intervention of a female restaurant patron, who uses the same phrase that June had used ineffectually with the black dogs—"*Ça suffit*" (108)—causes Jeremy to realize that, like the father, he is behaving like an "animal" (107), and he withdraws without doing any further harm to the man.

Jeremy's recognition of the distinct right of another human being to live despite the rightful emotions of "revenge and justice" (108) he has provoked is a step towards the ethical mode of being described by Lévinas, in which "to be in relation with the other face to face—is to be unable to kill." In *Black Dogs*, the violence associated, literally and symbolically, with the aftermath of the Second World War is neutralized, to a considerable extent, by the characters' ability to engage imaginatively with others. By using a first-person narrator openly characterized as a writer, McEwan is commenting on the role that authors can play in extending that engagement outwards to their readers. In *The Innocent*, on the other hand, the ethical relationship falters and violence prevails, partly owing to the failure of communication; in the end, Leonard and Maria are not capable of telling their stories clearly to one another, making true reconciliation impossible. In both novels, the burden of the past weighs heavily on the present, and can only be overcome by moving beyond old models of aggression, including totalitarianism and masculine domination, and by forming relationships "founded not on violence but on love."

6

ENDURING LOVE

While *The Innocent* and *Black Dogs* demonstrate respectively the urge towards self-absorption and a willingness to help others, *Enduring Love* begins by staging the conflict between those two impulses in highly dramatic form. The novel's opening scene, vividly portrayed in the film made of the book in 2004, involves a hot-air balloon accident in which a young boy is being carried away by high winds while his grandfather and five other men, including the narrator Joe Rose, attempt to save him. When the decision needs to be made between risking death by continuing to hang onto the ropes or letting go, all of the men except one, John Logan, a doctor who is also a father, decide to save themselves. As Joe later reflects, this incident exposes the primal impulses behind human society:

> Co-operation—the basis of our earliest hunting successes, the force behind our evolving capacity for language, the glue of our social cohesion . . . But letting go was in our nature too. Selfishness is also written on our hearts. This is our mammalian conflict—what to give to the others, and what to keep for yourself . . . . Hanging a few feet above the Chilterns escarpment, our crew enacted morality's ancient, irresolvable dilemma: us, or me. (14–5)

On one level, the novel makes clear that placing the needs of others over self-interest is the superior moral choice: Joe is haunted by the remorse of having "killed" (55) Logan, who falls to his death once the balloon, lightened in weight, is swept over the escarpment, while the doctor's heroism and masculine courage earn him great respect. The perverted nature of intense self-centeredness is presented through the character Jed Parry, one of the would-be rescuers, a young loner who suffers from a psychiatric disorder called de Clérambault's syndrome, which in his case takes the form of erotomania with religious and homosexual overtones that causes him to fall obsessively in love with Joe while totally disregarding Joe's own wishes.

Jed's stalking puts immense strain on Joe's marriage to Clarissa Mellon, a relationship that had flourished to that point because of open communication and loving attention to each other's needs, but which begins to collapse as each partner retreats into his or her own egocentric responses to the events following the accident. Like Bernard and June Tremaine in *Black Dogs*, Joe and Clarissa represent extreme positions divided along conventional gender lines. Joe, a writer of popular books about science, is a believer in the power of reason, convinced that all human behaviour can be explained by theories such as evolutionary psychology and genetics. Clarissa, an English professor specializing in Romantic literature, sees rationality as an insufficient way of understanding the world, since it breaks things down into "bits" (*EL* 71) to be analysed; she prefers a more synthetic vision, relying on feeling as well as thought, reaching beyond reason like John Keats's famous concept of "negative capability." While Joe is convinced that studying Jed's condition will be the solution to their problem, Clarissa suggests that her husband's rationality is akin to "a kind of innocence" (33) which, although usually endearing, under these extraordinary circumstances leads him to behave as obsessively as the man who is pursuing him. As Joe retreats into his research, he loses his ability to communicate with his wife, becoming "barely self-aware" (81) and unable to imagine things from her point of view. For her part, Clarissa does not take Joe's worries seriously, dismissing Jed as a harmless "Jesus freak" (57) whose homosexual affections will make a "funny story" (58) for Joe to tell his friends. Despite the conventional gender split of reason versus emotion, McEwan reverses the usual gender dynamic in terms of power. As in *The Comfort of Strangers*, McEwan here makes the man the object of desire; Joe, whose last name "Rose" has feminine connotations, takes on the typical female role of sexual victim, and is accused by Clarissa of leading Jed on, yet can get no one—neither his wife nor the police—to accept his fears as legitimate. Joe's isolation is exacerbated by his insecurities about his career; not having succeeded as a bona fide scientist, he thinks of himself as a "parasite" (75) living off other people's original ideas, and spends his time largely working alone at home, again in a more conventionally feminine position, while Clarissa has a doctorate and a full professional life at the university with students and colleagues who respect her. The gradual movement of Clarissa and Joe into separate and incommensurable states of mind underscores the lesson of the balloon incident that choosing selfishly to look after one's own needs while failing to recognize others' has destructive implications for human relationships.

Yet the thematization of ethical engagement in the novel is complicated by Joe's role as a first-person narrator. With the exception of a few letters written by Jed and Clarissa (and presumably selected by Joe for inclusion), the entire main narrative is told from Joe's perspective, even a chapter ostensibly designed to present Clarissa's point of view, albeit as "[Joe] later construed it" (79). Although Joe is a professional writer, there is no indication that what we are reading is one of the manuscripts he would normally produce for publication; rather, it seems to be a direct address to the reader, a rhetorical effort to draw us into the intricacies of his experiences and convince us of the rightness of his actions, despite the failure of Clarissa and his society at large, in the form of the police, to support him. In this respect, Joe's narration can be seen as a manifestation of the same "self-love" (19) that prompted him to save himself rather than hold onto the balloon. While John Logan may be regarded as heroic, his decision was self-destructive and ultimately pointless, since the balloon landed safely anyway with the boy unhurt; Joe, on the other hand, is alive, with the opportunity to shape his own story into any form he wishes, even one that finally represents him as possessing as much masculine bravery and self-sacrifice as Logan while apparently vindicating his original choice of self-preservation.

From the outset, Joe is highly self-conscious about the narrative that he is constructing, drawing attention to beginning, middle and ending with Aristotelian precision. The novel's opening sentence, "The beginning is simple to mark" (1), has overtones, as Peter Childs notes in his study of *Enduring Love*, of the biblical book of Genesis, with the country picnic about to be enjoyed by Joe and Clarissa as the Eden from which they are expelled by the death of the "falling man" (16) in combination with the entry of Jed as the "snake-like intruder" who destroys the loving innocence of their marriage (2007: 45). Joe marks the exact point that his life was changed forever as when he touched the wine bottle handed to him by Clarissa and he heard the shout of the trapped boy's grandfather; using literary and theatrical language to describe himself, he says that "At that moment a chapter, no, a whole stage of my life closed" (8). Yet despite Joe's claim of simplicity regarding this starting point, he proceeds to make it more complex, suggesting that the story could be seen to have begun with his and Clarissa's decision to have a picnic that day, or with the time or location of their rendezvous: "There are always antecedent causes," he notes. "A beginning is an artifice, and what recommends one over another is how much sense it makes of what follows" (17–8). This self-conscious reflection on act of narrative construction sounds remarkably similar to J. Hillis Miller's study *Reading Narrative*, in which he elaborates on the impossibility of fixing any point in a story as an absolute beginning. Clarissa, too, has her own starting point for her experience of the accident, and she and Joe weave their two stories into one, repeating traumatic elements and bringing their own perceptions to bear, including Clarissa's comparison of Logan's fall to the expulsion of Satan from Heaven in Milton's *Paradise Lost*. Together, Joe and Clarissa craft a story with "coherence" and "shape" (36), and are able to "tame" the horror of Logan's death "with words" (29) so that they seem confident that they can consider the incident finished and move on.

The balloon accident, however, quickly becomes just the opening episode of a much larger story, which comprises and is coterminous with the main text of *Enduring Love*. Unlike the story-within-the-story of the accident, this longer tale is not one that Joe constructs in partnership with Clarissa out of their shared experience, nor does it give him a sense of narrative mastery; rather, he feels isolated and undermined by a vague sense of "guilt and foreboding" (43). As with the balloon story, Joe is self-conscious about identifying the initiatory moment of this feeling, locating it not in the death of Logan but in the first phone call from Jed. The anxiety caused by this incident is evident in the fact that Joe lies about it twice—first, when he tells Clarissa that it is a wrong number; and second, when he informs Inspector Linley of the police that he discussed the call with his wife "the next morning" (156), not "two days" (217) later as she recalls and Joe's own narration confirms. Tellingly, Joe confides to his reader that concealing the identity of the caller was his "first serious mistake" (37), clearly considering it more reprehensible than his decision not to hold onto the rope. In fact, Joe is so unnerved by Jed's intrusion into his life that he grants it equal status to the balloon accident as a beginning for his story; once Jed's stalking becomes undeniable, Joe looks into the mirror and tries to imagine Jed's obsession: "This moment, as well as the one in the field when Clarissa handed me the bottle of wine, might serve as a starting point, for I think it was then that I really began to understand that this was not going to be over by the end of the day" (73). Joe's realization here is that he is in a "relationship" (73), and as Kiernan Ryan argues, Jed becomes Joe's "inverted mirror image" (2007: 52), the apparition of a latent homosexual desire that Joe does not want to acknowledge: "It was as if I had fallen through a crack in my own existence, down into another life, another set of sexual preferences" (*EL* 67). This alternative story is shadowed by the brief reference to Joe and Clarissa's neighbours, "a successful architect and his boyfriend," who keep an Edenic "fantasy garden" (54) on the roof of the apartment building.

The unease that Joe feels about this repressed desire becomes retroactively associated in his narrative with Logan's death. Before, Joe had been elated with his own survival; he "hugged [himself] tight" (19) in an almost erotic gesture of self-love when Logan's fate had become clear. Further, he felt his letting go of the rope was justifiable; he notes that "the child was not my child, and I was not going to die for it" (15), and explains to Clarissa simply that he and the others "tried to help and [they] failed" (33). Once the effect of Jed's initial phone call sets in, however, Joe "merge[s] it with all the trouble of the day before" (39). From that point on, Joe reinterprets his actions during the rescue attempt through the lens of his anxieties about his own manhood, which, as Ryan notes (2007: 50), existed prior to the accident owing to the lack of children in his marriage and his fears about Clarissa's fidelity, and which are no doubt deepened by his professional insecurities. Logan, the devoted father, successful doctor and amateur athlete, thus becomes the image of an ideal masculinity that Joe cannot live up to. Joe's ambivalence about Jed becomes subconsciously associated with his fear that Logan's wife Jean will accuse him of cowardice; he identifies his need to face what he expects to be her accusation of "murder" and to absolve himself in her eyes as the "centre" (122) of his story, without directly acknowledging the connection between the two sources of guilt.

As Sean Matthews points out (100), this declaration of remorse coincides with the exact middle of McEwan's book, just one indication of a homologous complicity between narrator and author that also reveals itself in Joe's open reflections on the persuasive effects of storytelling. Despite his proclaimed preference for scientific rationalism, Joe also admires the ability of literary narrative to be more believable than fact. Pondering a 1904 letter to the magazine *Nature* about a dog that seemingly tricks its master into giving up his chair, Joe thinks, "What I liked here was how the power and attractions of narrative had clouded judgement. By any standards of scientific enquiry the story, however charming, was a nonsense" (41). With this admission, Joe moves away from his entrenched rationalism to a worldview much closer to that of the more imaginative Clarissa and her mentor Professor Jocelyn Kale, who concur about the value of patently made-up stories such as William Wordsworth's legendary put-down of Keats; Kale remarks, "It isn't true, but we need it. A kind of myth," and Clarissa adds, "It isn't true, but it tells the truth" (169).

To re-establish Joe's believability as an honest narrator, not prone to literary fabrication, McEwan later has him reject his earlier attraction to scientific anecdote: "Narrative—my gut tightened at the word. What balls I had written the night before" (56). Joe even claims to forego the creation of an artificially happy ending to describe the scene after he has saved the abducted Clarissa from Jed's violent intentions:

> In a world in which logic was the engine of feeling, this should have been the moment when Clarissa stood, when we moved towards each other and folded into each other's arms with kisses and tears .... But such logic would have been inhuman .... The narrative compression of storytelling, especially in the movies, beguiles us with happy endings into forgetting that sustained stress is corrosive of feeling. (213)

This gesture towards psychological realism, however, is undercut by other aspects of the ending of Joe's narrative, which show clear signs of literary influence.

In constructing the end of his story, not only does Joe place himself in the role as masculine rescuer of the finally passive and victimized Clarissa, he also manages symbolically to recover the traumatic losses of his story's beginning. As Childs notes (2007: 119), the final picnic engineered by Joe to explain to Jean Logan why there was a woman in the car with her husband the day of the accident typologically redeems both Joe and Clarissa's picnic and the rotting picnic lunch found in Logan's car. The revelation of the affair between Logan's passengers, the fatuous James Reid, ironically the Euler Professor of Logic, and his vacuous student Bonny Deedes, restores the unassailability of John Logan's marital fidelity while serving also to displace onto someone less threatening the charge of professorial misconduct associated with Clarissa, whom Joe had suspected of having an affair with "some hot little bearded fuck-goat of a post-graduate" (105). Joe describes Jean's desperate pleas for forgiveness from her wrongly accused dead husband as "almost mad, Mad Hatterish, here on the river bank where Lewis Carroll, the Dean of Christ Church, had once entertained the darling objects of his own obsessions" (230), subtly recasting his narrative's focus on sexual perversion into the context of a children's story, a trip through the looking glass completed with the resumption of normative heterosexual family life. At the same time, Clarissa's dream of having her own children is brought to life through her game with Jean's daughter Rachael, in which the girl frees herself from being tickled by knowing Clarissa's "secret" name, "Rumpelstiltskin" (224), the fairy tale reference invoking the magical possibility of saving a child from being cruelly taken from its parents, as Clarissa's children were taken from her by the surgery that left her sterile. While Clarissa reclaims her lost role as mother through the affections of Rachael and her brother Leo, Joe, too, recovers his paternity, ending his narrative hand-in-hand with both children, replacing their absent father and entertaining them with an imaginative story about the water molecules in the river, "bound together by a mysterious powerful force" (225). The resolution of Joe's narrative thus recalls his attraction to the power of scientific anecdote, which can "cloud judgement" and be more compelling than fact; its "logic" is the "engine of feeling," as Joe draws on fairy tale and conventional comic motifs to fabricate an end that is overtly artificial.

As Kiernan Ryan suggests, Joe's self-consciousness about his role in constructing his story paradoxically tends to make readers accept him as a credible narrator: "We are disposed to trust him precisely because he stresses the arbitrariness and subjectivity of his account" (2007: 47). Joe's narrative manipulation, while self-serving, is at the same time proof of his honesty, since he does not attempt to deceive readers into believing there has been no manipulation of the facts. David Malcolm too notes that "The reader is meant to feel at ease about Joe's account, and to believe and trust him" (161). Joe's trustworthiness as narrator is heightened by the fact that he is "continually fretting at the difficulties he has in telling his own story" (Matthews 95), including acknowledging the possibility that he is a victim of self-deception, an effect of the evolutionary heritage that makes people unconscious purveyors of believable fictions: "We're descended from the indignant, passionate tellers of half truths who in order to convince others, simultaneously convinced themselves" (*EL* 181). Joe surmises that this human tendency to "self-persuasion" (104) interferes with our empirical understanding of the world, such that subjective interpretation colours our apprehension of things: "Believing is seeing" (181).

Joe is aware, for instance, that his perceptions of the events at a restaurant late in the novel when Jed hires hit men to kill him are distorted. At first, his mind leaps to create explanations that could account for the two oddly dressed men who approach a neighbouring table: "A variety of possibilities unspooled before me at speed: a student stunt; vendors . . . some new version of the kissogram" (171). The confusion at the scene is not just visual but also auditory; other witnesses tell the police that they heard one of the men speak in either Arabic or French (180); here, McEwan is evoking Edgar Allan Poe's seminal detective story "Murders in the Rue Morgue", in which witnesses give conflicting reports of different languages spoken by the murderer in that case, which turns out to be an orang-utan. When the shooting begins in the restaurant, the violence is so shocking that it exceeds rational understanding, much like the mystery at the heart of Poe's tale; Joe recalls, "I did not believe what I was seeing" (172). Later, when he describes what he witnessed to the police, he reverts to his literary inclinations, purposely creating a scenario that he knows to be false: he claims to have taken a few bites of his dessert when the shooting began, while the waiter has told the police that he had not yet set the dishes down. Joe asks the reader outright, "But exactly what interests of mine were served by my own account of the restaurant lunch?" (181).

Matthews cites this admission of wilful misrepresentation as an example of just one of seven types of narratorial unreliability in the novel, including "*deliberate*" (95), as in this case, and "*uncanny*," in which "elements of the narrative . . . 'break frame', constituting forces within the story which disrupt or undermine its own plausibility" (98–99, italics in original). Joe's identification of the flavour of his ice cream to Inspector Wallace as "apple" (181) when he has already described it to the reader as "lime, just to the green side of white" (171) could be seen, as Adam Mars-Jones notes in his review of the novel, a sort of self-conscious "gimmick" (1999: 1) on McEwan's part; or it could be evidence of a frame-breaking pattern visible in the text, a repetition of the Edenic fall motif introduced with the opening picnic, which carries through to the "two apples" (*EL* 115) found in the bag in Logan's car and the final revelation of knowledge and restoration of innocence in the novel's ending.

Matthews' categories of unreliability extend from the deliberate or conscious, to the uncanny or unconscious, to the "*psychotic*," which includes aspects of the text that raise "concerns about the narrator's own sanity" (102, italics in original). These elements range from Joe's own fears that he is behaving like a "mental patient" (*EL* 58) to his growing similarities to the mentally ill Jed, who serves as form of dark "parody" (63, 128) of "rational Joe" (83), or perhaps even a projection of his own psychic instability, what Clarissa calls "a spirit of [his] dislocated, incomplete character" (102). Taking Jed as a manifestation of Joe's deranged mind rather than a disturbed person in his own right would mean that Joe's narration, as Malcolm suggests, is nothing more than "an extensive piece of lying" (179) with no verisimilar qualities whatsoever. Matthews argues that such an approach would lead to "an extreme, even perverse reading of *Enduring Love*" (104), especially given the seemingly incontrovertible evidence of Jed's illness given in the case study from the *British Review of Psychiatry* that appears in the text as Appendix I. Rather, Matthews, like Malcolm and other critics, not only contends that accepting Joe's sanity is a precondition to any meaningful interpretation of the novel, but also notes that we as readers "must somehow take account of both his right-ness *and* his unreliability" (105), and come to terms with how that contradiction reflects on and undermines the stability of our own readerly practices.

The crucial question of narratorial sanity and its effects on reading brings to mind Shoshana Felman's famous essay on Henry James's *The Turn of the Screw*, "Turning the Screw of Interpretation", which begins by citing the critical divide caused by the 1934 essay "The Ambiguity of Henry James", in which Edmund Wilson draws on Freudian theory to suggest that the governess in James's novella is a sexually repressed hysteric who projects her desires in the form of ghosts and possessed children. This groundbreaking essay led to the formation of two critical camps—the Freudians and the anti-Freudians (i.e., those who believe the governess to be sane and the ghosts real)—which, as Felman describes, act out the ambiguity at the heart of the text in their attempts to arrive at an interpretation that would definitively silence those on the oppo-site side. In Felman's view, these adversarial critics overlook "the very textuality of the text":

> The question, therefore, can no longer be simply to decide whether in effect the "Freudian" reading is true or false, correct or incorrect .... A new, far more troubling question can no longer be avoided ... is a reading of *ambiguity* as such really *possible*? Is it at all possible to read and to interpret ambiguity *without reducing it* in the very process of interpretation? Are reading and ambiguity in any way *compatible*? (117)

Instead of trying "to *capture* the mystery's solution" (119) and nar-row the text's equivocal passages to a single meaning, Felman proposes that a more productive approach is to examine the ways in which James's novella contains within itself structures that produce and reflect on the novella's complex effects on its reader-ship. These embedded acts of narrating, writing and interpreting include the relating, through a frame narrative, of the history of the creation and transmission of the governess's manuscript and its oral presentation to a group of listeners; there is also the text's fascination with the circulation of letters, the contents of which remain hidden from the reader. Felman sees in the letters and the ghosts a "double mystery" (149) central to the novella's organiza-tion, since the ghosts, too, are indecipherable texts, "ambiguous and contradictory signifiers" (154) eliciting attempts at interpretation. By looking closely at these self-reflexive elements of writing, storytelling and reading, Felman suggests, we can "understand the necessity and the rhetorical functioning of the textual ambiguity," not asking the question "'*what* does the story mean?' but rather '*how* does the story mean?'" (119).

As we have seen, unlike *The Turn of the Screw*, *Enduring Love* has not evoked division among its critics, since Joe's sanity is taken as irrefutable. McEwan's novel has, however, produced a "*reading-effect*" (Felman 126, italics in original) similar to James's text in that it creates a tension between narratorial believability and unreliability that critics struggle to resolve in their various readings. This elusive point of interpretive reconciliation functions as a missing or repressed text that is figured in different ways within the novel itself. As in *The Turn of the Screw*, there are embedded in *Enduring Love* structures and motifs that call attention to the processes of writing and reading, and especially of interpretation, the putting into words of meanings just below the surface of understanding.

Despite Joe's dismissal of the "talking cure"—"A genteel fraud, in my view" (99)—his tale bears a remarkable resemblance to the psychoanalytic narrative known as "transference," with the reader in the position of "analyst" (Childs 110). As Felman reminds us, the idea of transference was introduced in Sigmund Freud's *The Interpretation of Dreams*, in which he theorized that unconscious desires "transferred" or projected onto the images in our dreams, creating a symbolic text that can be analysed. Joe describes his experiences several times in oneiric terms: Logan's death recalls to him a recurring nightmare from his youth in which he fails to rescue helpless people during disasters, Jed appears to him to be "the stuff of bad dreams" (147), and so on. Further, there are clear signs of repressed anxieties attached to transitory images, such as "the flash of a white shoe and something red" (42) that Joe sees in the library, fuelling his dread of being stalked.

The process of interpreting the symbols of Joe's unconscious fears into forms intelligible to others is captured in the words "curtain" and "signal," which haunt his memory "like an enduring fragment of a childhood dream" (89). These binary signifiers, which convey both concealment and expression or revelation, create "associations" for Joe "that lay just off the screen of recall"

(89), so that he must "hope that stronger associations would break through, perhaps in [his] sleep" (100). The fact that he remembers seeing "curtain" in his own handwriting (89), though the more likely source is his "black labelled box jammed with clippings" (92), suggests that the word has personal, deep-seated significance. Joe's eventual connection of these terms with the original case history of de Clérambault's syndrome, in which a French woman became convinced that King George the Fifth was communicating with her through signals made with his palace window curtains "that she alone could read" (124), is itself an act of reading, an internal reflection of our interpretive work of uncovering the hidden meanings of Joe's story.

Similarly, the catastrophic event of Logan's death functions in the text as a *mise en abyme* of the act of signification. As we have seen, the incident forms the basis for the story created jointly by Joe and Clarissa as they attempt to master the terror of what they have witnessed. On a more figural level, though, Joe's response to the doctor's demise reveals the difficulty of expressing in language that which is inherently unrepresentable, what Slavoj Žižek, following Freud and Jacques Lacan, calls "das Ding," the "traumatic element at [the] very heart" of the symbolic order (1989: 133). From the outset, the accident is associated with emptiness; Joe's first mention of the balloon distinguishes it from "the nominal space that encloses a cartoon character's speech or thought" (3), but he goes on to describe Logan's being swept away to die as "a stunt, a joke, a cartoon," "the kind of thing that happened to Bugs Bunny, or Tom, or Jerry" (15). During and after his fall, Logan becomes a "stick" (16, 23) figure, a caricature rather than a human being, and the feeling of "*absence*" (23, italics in original) that emanates from his shattered corpse is a sign of the "obliterated self" (Ryan 2007: 51). This absolute negation of being has repeated manifestations throughout the text—in the skeletal Jed, about whom Joe thinks, "It was almost as if he didn't exist" (147); and in the assassins in the restaurant, whose faces, covered with latex masks, are "the colour of no one's skin," with "a robotic nullity of expression" (171). Joe's efforts throughout his narration to put into words this "traumatic kernel" of the Real enact the "symbolization/historicization" (Žižek 1989: 133, 135) that Žižek sees as the effect of the symbolic order, a signifying process that culminates in a second event that gives retroactive meaning to the original loss. Žižek likens this "accomplishment of symbolic destiny" (1989: 135) to the kinds of "second death[s]" (1989: 134) experienced by cartoon characters such as Tom and Jerry, who step off precipices but do not fall until they look down and see that they are walking on air. In Joe's case, the traumatic ordeal of Logan's death, with its associated guilt for having killed him, is not fully real to Joe until it is repeated in the form of Jed's prospective murder, which Joe prepares for by buying an illegal firearm. In order to reach this point of symbolic fruition, Joe literally works his way through the alphabet of his "Domesday Book" (184) of former acquaintances, searching for a criminal contact, towards the terminal letter that will spell the fulfillment of his horror and remorse.

Just as Logan's death represents an absent reality that must be signified in order to be understood, so too does the missing letter from Keats to Fanny Brawne sought by Clarissa function as a symbol of the processes of interpretation central to *Enduring Love*. As with the letters in *The Turn of the Screw*, the contents of this document, which may or may not exist, are never revealed and can merely be guessed at by both the reader and Clarissa. Like her non-existent children, the letter is undelivered, a ghostly and ambiguous presence that invites speculation.

In this respect, the missing letter plays a role in the text similar to that of Jed, who is frequently described as a phantom and who becomes the focus of intense hermeneutic activity. For his part, Jed is a deficient reader, since he perceives in the world, and particularly in Joe, only what his madness leads him to see; Joe notes, "Nothing could prove him wrong, nothing was needed to prove him right" (143). Clarissa, on the other hand, whose name implies clarity and who is a literary critic, should be more adept at analysis, yet fails to recognize what is in front of her and mistakes Jed's actions as comic. (Clarissa's generic misreading of Jed is in contrast with Jean's interpretation of her husband's death, which she wrongly assumes includes the sordid tragedy of infidelity.) Rather than believing Joe about what he is enduring, Clarissa forces him to "evince the evidence" (48), as he does with his science writing, creating within the text a parallel activity to the interpretive work being done by the reader.

Despite the ultimate indisputability of Jed's mental illness, the proofs that Joe provides to Clarissa and others are difficult to verify and frequently misconstrued. Clarissa doubts Jed's physical presence, since she does not see him lurking near the apartment: " 'Joe!' She shouted. 'You say he's outside, but when I go out there's no one' " (148). Since Joe erases Jed's many phone messages, they become unreadable texts, much like the Keats letter. Jed's correspondence to Joe should serve as literal representations of his actions, yet they raise different suspicions in Clarissa's mind: she remarks that the handwriting is "rather like" (100) Joe's, implying that he has written the letters himself, whether deliberately or unconsciously. The police seem to accept that the author of the letters is someone other than Joe, but are incapable of piecing together the ambiguities and inconsistencies in Jed's prose. Joe expects Inspector Linley to perform the work of a literary critic to see the threats—"They're not right out front. You'll need to read carefully," (156), he advises—but as Inspector Wallace later reminds Joe, even "educated people" like "book writers" cannot "get the record straight" (179) about matters they should know well, such as the conflict between Wordsworth and Keats. In fact, the kind of intellectual work that Joe feels is needed to make his case through textual evidence is held in low esteem in the world of *Enduring Love*: both Clarissa and Jean, who is also an academic, are overworked members of an undervalued profession, constantly facing monetary cuts.

While Joe is unable to convince others of the threat to him through textual means, Jed's physical violence should be less susceptible to misinterpretation. The attempt on Joe's life at the restaurant, though, is still open to alternative readings: the man mistaken for Joe, Colin Tapp, is also a target for international terrorists, reversing the earlier scenario when Joe had identified himself with Yvonne Fletcher, a policewoman killed by a Libyan sniper, by standing where she stood when she was shot (44). Jed's abduction and confinement of Clarissa in the apartment is a seemingly unambiguous sign that Joe has been right all along; even she finally appears to believe what her husband has been telling her, saying to Jed, "He was actually very frightened of you, you know, standing outside the house, and all the letters" (211). Yet despite admitting that she had been "completely wrong" (216) in her final letter to Joe, Clarissa still assigns most of the blame for the situation to him, claiming that Jed might have been "deflected" (218) from his mad behaviour if Joe had not encouraged him.

Within the main narrative of *Enduring Love*, then, the interpretive work of the characters, paralleling our own reading activity,
establishes Joe's sanity and Jed's insanity persuasively, though not
incontrovertibly, given Clarissa's lingering doubts. The supposedly definitive pieces of evidence appear after the main narrative,
as appendices from the author to which the reader has privileged access; the case study from *The British Review of Psychiatry*
and Jed's letter from the asylum expressing his undaunted love
for Joe respectively provide a rationalist perspective on, and an
irrational demonstration of, Jed's erotomania. As was recognized
fairly quickly after the novel's publication, though, the case study
is a hoax and the last names of its putative authors, Drs Robert
Wenn and Antonio Camia, are an anagram for Ian McEwan (Miller
1999: 1). Ryan marks this as the most telling instance of the complicity between the author and his narrator, "whose first-person
account of events he has buttressed with fabricated evidence"
(2007: 46). The misleading nature of the appendices is reinforced
by McEwan's pointed insertion of "Acknowledgements," with no
mention of the psychiatric journal, at the very end, which serves
to "realign [the appendices] as components of the novel's fictive
world" (Ryan 2007: 46).

McEwan's use of the case study recalls the appearance in John
Fowles's *The French Lieutenant's Woman* of a partly made-up text-
book account of the nineteenth-century trial of Lieutenant Emile
de la Roncière, an officer convicted of sexually assaulting Marie de
Morell, the 16-year-old daughter of his commanding officer. The
evidence against La Roncière included insulting letters supposedly
in his own handwriting, but apparently forged by Marie herself,
who also wounded herself; according to the real-life contemporary German physician Karl Matthaei, pages of whose booklet
Fowles reproduces in translation, Marie was a model of female
hysterical behaviour, unconsciously tricking others because of
repressed sexual desire. The case history in *The French Lieutenant's
Woman* is meant to help Charles Smithson see through the irrational game-playing of Sarah Woodruff, but instead drives him
deeper into infatuation. As I have argued elsewhere (Wells 2003),
The French Lieutenant's Woman has embedded within it the terms
of its seduction of its own readership, which it achieves through
a combination of overt self-consciousness and compelling narrative believability. Similarly, McEwan's inclusion of the appendices

provides convincing proof of Joe's ultimate reliability as a narrator while at the same time calling attention to the utter fictiveness of his tale.

The tension between Joe's egocentric, first-person control of the story, and the reader's irresistible attraction to the narrative's ambiguities and points of textual self-consciousness produces a complex reading-effect that is central to *Enduring Love*. McEwan challenges us to produce stable meaning from a text that goes out of its way to foreground its own narrative construction, to simulate our own work as critics through the internal representation of interpretive acts, and to complicate the role of narratorial voice. The resulting relationship between text and reader is fraught with conflict and cooperation, much like the novel's dramatic opening scene, leaving us, as Matthews suggests, questioning "what is at stake in *our* reading" (105) of Joe's tale.

7

AMSTERDAM AND *ON CHESIL BEACH*

Written almost a decade apart, these two short novels—*Amsterdam* (1998) and *On Chesil Beach* (2007)—have a number of things in common despite their very different subjects and generic styles. Both focus on a small number of characters engaged in tightly formed relationships that lead to intense dramatic action and climactic endings; in fact, each is constructed in five clear sections or "acts", with, as Peter Childs notes about *Amsterdam*, "the rhythm of a play and the feel of a script in the making" (2006: 118). In an interview, McEwan said that he hoped his readers would enjoy "almost a kind of theatrical experience" (*Bold Type Interview*), a statement that could easily be extended to *On Chesil Beach*, which has also been described as being like a musical composition in five movements (*Out of the Book*). *Amsterdam*, "part psychological novel and part social satire" (Malcolm 194), centers on an escalating conflict between two friends who reunite at the funeral of mutual former lover and end up murdering one another: Clive Linley, a composer, and Vernon Halliday, a tabloid editor, both of whom are ruthlessly self-promoting. In a scene rife with allusions to the Romantic period with its reverence for the male poetic genius, Clive puts his own artistic success above human life by ignoring a woman about to be raped. Vernon, a capitalist whose unfeeling exploitation of others leads to a literal loss of bodily sensation, chooses to publish compromising photos of a prominent right-wing politician. Both men are products of their social context: urban Britain under a waning neo-Conservative government, with all the attributes of unchecked greed and ambition, rampant commercialism, social decay and environmental degradation familiar from McEwan's other texts set during the Thatcher era, *The Child in Time* and *The Ploughman's Lunch*.

McEwan has claimed that writing *Amsterdam* was his relieved "farewell" (*Bold Type Interview*) to the detrimental years of Conservative rule, which ended in 1997 with the defeat of Prime Minister John Major's government; the novel, a tightly constructed comic satire in the tradition of Evelyn Waugh and Kingsley Amis, gave McEwan the opportunity to level his final critique and end by properly punishing his representative villains. *On Chesil Beach*, on the other hand, is a "period piece" (Alvarez 2) set in 1962, just before Britain entered the "swinging Sixties." The main characters Florence Ponting, a promising violinist terrified by intercourse, and her new husband, history student Edward Mayhew, eager for sexual experience, have no socially acceptable way of communicating with one another, and their disastrous wedding night in a coastal hotel in Dorset enacts the collision of more repressive times with modern liberation. In both books, the characters are either unwilling or unable to recognize the needs of others, and remain trapped within modes of self-serving behaviour that ultimately harm them as well. As in so much of McEwan's work, gender is crucial in these texts, with the men having greater access to power and knowledge in both periods, and the women struggling to adapt to changing roles that only slowly compensate for their historical disadvantage.

Molly Lane, whose funeral forms the opening scene of *Amsterdam*, seems in many respects to have been a liberated woman, treated as an equal by the men who knew her. At various times a restaurant critic or a columnist for *Vogue*, Molly, whose name invokes the voluptuous wife in James Joyce's *Ulysses*, led an independent life, having several relationships, including one with Clive, who valued her sexual energy and her advice on music and food, and another with Vernon, who enjoyed her companionship, remembering fondly that she taught him "all about porcini, picking them, cooking them" (8). They both recall her as a "lovely girl" who "danced naked on Christmas Eve on a snooker table in a Scottish castle," staging an "Adam and Eve tableau" with a "cue rest for a snake and a red ball for an apple" (7), yet who was more than just an erotic spectacle for them, always demanding "Lie still, look at me, really *look* at me" (15). She was able to see people beyond their social exteriors and accept them with compassion and good humour, as demonstrated by her photographs of the cross-dressing of Conservative Foreign Secretary Julian Garmony, a secret she would have continued to keep if not for the sudden onset of her fatal illness, which robbed her of her independence and made her "the sick-room prisoner of her morose, possessive husband" (3) George Lane, the publisher of *The Judge*, the newspaper edited by Vernon.

Molly's demise, brought on by what seems to be a stroke, was preceded by a failure of language that symbolizes a general collapse of moral meaning and goodness in the world of the text. Once Molly could no longer remember "bed, cream, mirror" (3), simple words associated with her identity, she was on the verge of a total silencing that removed her compassionate influence from the heartless society around her. This loss is recognized by the third-person narrator, focalized through Clive's point of view: "There was something seriously wrong with the world for which neither God nor his absence could be blamed. Man's first disobedience, the Fall, a falling figure, an oboe, nine notes, ten notes" (4). The Biblical image of the Fall, used by McEwan in other texts such as *The Child in Time* and *Enduring Love*, here is connected to Molly's turn as a coyly knowing Eve, as well as to the description of the crematorium, "The Garden of Remembrance," a degraded Eden with "savagely cut" plants and "flattened cigarette butts" (4) strewn on the grass. The frigid temperature at the funeral, "minus eleven" (4), brings to mind the elegiac 1940 poem "In Memory of W.B. Yeats"—"What instruments we have agree / The day of his death was a dark cold day" (197)—in which W.H. Auden laments the passing of a brilliant poetic voice and warns of the dangers of hatred between individuals and violence between nations.

With Molly's death, the world depicted in *Amsterdam* loses the benign "feminine" principle of caring for others, and except for Clive and Vernon's remembrances of her, women play little role for the first three sections of the novel. Clive's current love interest, Susie Marcellan, lives in New York, and Vernon's wife Mandy, whom he cheats on, barely appears in the text. There are occasional parts illustrating women's general powerlessness, such as the "dyslexic sub" at the newspaper whom Vernon had promised to "stand by" (44) but let get fired anyway. Most of the action, though, involves the egotistical male characters Clive and Vernon, and their progress towards mutual self-destruction, foreshadowed by the epigraph from Auden's "The Crossroads"—"The friends who met here and embraced are gone, / Each to his own mistakes"—and carried forward by the inexorable plotting of McEwan's narrative.

As a musician, Clive joins other figures in McEwan's work such as authors Stephen Lewis in *The Child in Time* and Briony Tallis in *Atonement* who provide internalized textual reflections on aesthetic theory and practice and the ethical role of artists in society. A well-recognized composer in mid-career, Clive has been branded an "arch-conservative" by some for his traditional musical style, yet praised for the accessibility of his art: "All agreed that along with Schubert and McCartney, Linley could write a melody" (21). This endorsement earned him the commission to compose a symphony to herald the millennium four years hence, a work with commercial appeal designed to " 'play itself' into public consciousness" (21) through repeated use on the television news. Clive's skill in creating popular pieces stems from his rejection of the modernist aesthetic, with its "atonal and aleatoric music, tone rows, electronics, the disintegration of pitch into sound" (21), which he sees as the product of theoreticians and academics, art that is "jealously professionalised, isolated and rendered sterile, its vital covenant with a general public arrogantly broken" (22). By contrast, Clive strives "to reassert music's essential communicativeness," to return it to the "humanistic tradition" (22) from which it originated as a natural form of human expression and interaction.

It is curious, therefore, that Clive, with few exceptions, strongly dislikes other human beings and prefers to retreat to artistic solitude. At the funeral, he is "invigorated" by "a jolt of misanthropy" (9) and longs to escape to his warm, quiet studio; when he gets there, though, he is troubled by a persistent tingling in his left hand, not only an after-effect of the cold that numbed all the funeral-goers, but also a symbol of his moral impairment, connected to Molly's paralysis before death, which he fears will be his own fate. The fact that the numbness is restricted to his left hand also points to the "sinister" (in the etymological sense of that word) side of his nature. The potential for monstrousness in Clive is reinforced by the image of his limping along a railway platform on his way to the Lake District with "an unevenness in his stride, as though one leg had grown longer than the other" (63), caused by his having stepped on someone's discarded chewing gum, another situation that elicits a misanthropic response.

Clive hopes that by escaping from London to the countryside he can seclude himself in a landscape "bleached" of "human meaning" and receive inspiration for his symphony from the sublime experience of nature: "The unimaginable age of the mountains and the fine mesh of living things that lay across them would remind him that he was part of this order and insignificant within it, and he would be set free" (78). The corruption of the fallen world of the city, though, is rapidly spreading to the pristine countryside, a sign of the creeping decay of contemporary society, so that Clive is disturbed by the "visual pollution" of a nearly hundred schoolchildren in "day-glo anoraks," "trampl[ing]" the "beauty spot" (83) and spoiling his concentration. Still, he is inspired by the song of a bird that he believes will provide the final melody for his work, a creative discovery that will be testament to his status as a "genius," a title that he at first rejects owing to the "arrogance" (62) of those who assume it for themselves (especially novelists, as McEwan slyly takes a dig at himself through his character), but later mistakenly accepts as deserved.

Through the passage set in the Lake District, McEwan draws a clear connection between Clive and the Romantic poets who found inspiration there, such as Percy Bysshe Shelley and William Wordsworth. Like them, Clive sees the solitary artist working in communion with nature as the highest form of creativity. As Anne K. Mellor points out in "Why Women Didn't Like Romanticism", however, this artistic figure from the nineteenth century also is associated with a "powerful egotism at the core of romantic ideology" (284), which endows individual poets with the god-like power to be "the unacknowledged legislators of the world," in Percy Shelley's phrase from his "Defence of Poetry." In this role, the Romantic poets, almost exclusively male, were concerned most with the process of creation, which was itself revolutionary and liberating, but less with the products of their work, which were only "dead thoughts" (Shelley's 'Ode to the West Wind', qtd. in Mellor 282) once they became words on the page. For Mary Shelley, Mellor explains, this attitude was frightening in that it relieved poets of responsibility for the bloody social upheaval caused by their ideas in places such as post-Revolution France, the horrible effects of which she symbolized in the form of the creature in her novel *Frankenstein*: "The failure of the masculine romantic ideology to care for the created product as much as for the creative process, together with its implicit assumption that the ends can justify the means, can produce a romanticism that, as Mary Shelley showed, is truly *monstrous*" (285–6). As an alternative model, Mary Shelley advocated a more feminine "ethical vision" (285) that involved taking responsibility for all of one's creations, including children, who, along with wives and lovers such as Mary herself, were often neglected and treated badly by the male artists.

McEwan openly parodies the Romantic masculine worldview through Clive, who, when faced with the decision to prolong his moment of inspiration or help a woman whom he watches being assaulted down the hillside, chooses to privilege his art. The ethical significance of this key event in the novel is heightened by its being clearly staged as a dramatic scene for Clive and the reader to watch and react to; he sees the woman and her assailant "as if they were actors striking up a tableau whose meaning he was supposed to guess" (85). Although the woman escapes, Clive makes no police report the same attacker is free to rape another victim, leading Vernon to berate his friend for neglecting his "moral duty" and not recognizing that "there are certain things more important than symphonies. They're called people" (119).

While Vernon's high dudgeon seems reasonable, it conceals the fact that he ignored Clive's earlier attempt to describe what he had witnessed because he was preoccupied with his plans to publish the photos of Garmony's transvestism. Through Vernon's capitalist excesses, McEwan levels a critique of popular or "low" culture as devastating as that on elite or "high" culture through Clive's lust for personal fame. Vernon, who got his first big break as a journalist by accidentally uncovering a story about an American president's exorbitant hair implant procedure (likely suggested to McEwan by President Bill Clinton's notorious haircut on Airforce One in 1993), thrives in the high-stakes world of tabloid journalism, with its scandals, scoops and sensationalism. In the predominantly masculine setting of the newsroom, Vernon is the master of his domain, presiding over a pseudo-democracy where everyone's input is solicited though not really heeded, and where he must guard against the machinations of pretenders to his position, such as the "Cassius"-like (39) deputy foreign editor, Frank Dibben. Outside that competitive environment, though, his identity loses coherence; the narrator describes him as "simply the sum of all the people who had listened to him . . . . He was widely known as a man without edges, without faults or virtues as a man who did not fully exist" (30). When Vernon loses all sensation in the right side of his head, which includes the part of the brain often associated with emotional intelligence, he accepts this as a sign of his "non-existence" (31), but it is also a physical manifestation of the same moral paralysis that afflicts Clive after Molly's death. Vernon is brought to life by the opportunity for power and profit opened up by the revelation of the salacious photos by George Lane, who wants revenge on Garmony for sleeping with his wife. Notwithstanding Vernon's rationalization that he is publishing the pictures to save the nation from Garmony's right-wing agenda, his real motivations are completely self-serving, putting "circulation figures" (120) over people, as Clive perceptively points out.

The counter-weight to Vernon's bid to exploit the Foreign Secretary's private life comes in the form of Rose Garmony, the only major female character who actually appears in the text. Introduced at the beginning of the "fourth act," Rose revives the feminine principle of benevolence lost with Molly's death, though in a compromised form reflective of the society's general debasement. Like John Logan in *Enduring Love* and Henry Perowne in *Saturday*, Rose is a doctor, a figure associated in McEwan's work with professional probity and a commitment to helping others. As a surgeon, she saves small children, and she is connected to symbols of maternal fecundity, including the "basket of pineapples, mangoes and grapes" (93) brought as an offering by the worried father of a young female patient. Rose knows how to manipulate her own image, however, to her own advantage, staging the press conference at which she declares her support for her husband at the family's country home, a pastoral setting recalling that fallen Eden in the novel's opening scene and highlighting Julian's plight as sacrificial "lamb" (122), embraced and forgiven by his wife and children. Rose's carefully crafted tag lines—that Vernon Halliday has "the moral stature of a flea" (125) and that "love was a greater force than spite" (124)—are obviously constructed as sound bites for maximum effect with the media.

While Rose's calculated intervention with the press saves her husband's position, at least temporarily, it does not succeed in infusing the world of the text with a new sense of moral direction. Rose is hailed for being " 'the new supportive wife' who had her own corner *and* fought her husband's corner" (127), echoing the praise Hillary Clinton received for supporting her husband Bill during the Gennifer Flowers affair; although this suggests greater respect for women's influence, Rose's moment in the spotlight is quickly followed by the new editor of *The Judge*, Frank Dibben, directing his staff to hire "someone of low to medium intelligence, possibly female" (129), to write trivial human interest stories. Vernon, sacked by the paper for his failure to handle the Garmony situation correctly, directs his fury at Clive, who has been berating him for betraying Molly's privacy by publishing the photos and questioning his professional ethics; Clive, for his part, finds his inspiration ruined by Vernon's threat to inform the police of his friend's refusal to report the assault he witnessed, and ends up producing a symphony that is painfully unoriginal. The two men move relentlessly towards a climax of assured mutual destruction, much like the Siamese twins covered by *The Judge* who have "bite marks" (37) on each of their faces. Their pact to help each other in the event of incapacitation, reached after Molly's illness, was intended as a gesture of true friendship; instead, it becomes their method of revenge against one another that leads paradoxically to their own deaths, as they trick each other into agreeing to euthanasia in Amsterdam, where mercy killing has been decriminalized. Unable to move because of the sedatives they have slipped into each other's drinks, Vernon and Clive finally achieve a total paralysis equal to Molly's, and her appearances in each of their dying visions—accusing Clive for not helping "her" when she was in distress in the Lake District, and cheating on Vernon with his nemesis Frank—are only illusory returns of the feminine principle of morality. The novel's scene shows us an unredeemed society, with George Lane relishing the defeat of his wife's former lovers and his political enemy Garmony, enjoying the benefits of his ill-gotten profits, and preparing to ask Vernon's widow out on a date.

Unlike the morally degraded 1990s London in *Amsterdam*, the early 1960s Britain depicted in *On Chesil Beach* is in a state of cultural transition, caught between traditional English standards of duty and respectability and the values associated with an

increasingly dominant United States, including the political ideal-
ism of the Kennedy era, looser sexual mores, and commercialism,
with "an avalanche of TVs, cars, supermarkets and other junk"
(31), all made in America, pouring into Europe. The post-war waning of Britain as an international power is a familiar subject from
other McEwan texts such as *The Ploughman's Lunch* and *The Innocent*; in this case, the central characters, Edward and Florence, seem
poised to thrive in the new world order: "The sixties was their first
decade of adult life, and it surely belonged to them" (25). Florence,
a talented and confident musician, is on her way to a successful
career; Edward has been offered employment by his new father-in-
law, nepotism still being a perquisite of their patriarchal society,
but he plans to keep up his writing, significantly about the roles
of individuals in the grand sweep of history. Blessed with talent,
education, employment and supportiveness for each other's pur-
suits, Florence and Edward represent a renewed sense of British
promise, symbols of "a modern country where there was equality
and things actually got done" (25) being dreamed into being by a
fresh generation of political leaders.

Yet while the newly married couple has everything they should
need for a prosperous future together, including genuine love
for one another, there are many impediments to their happiness.
Their relationship, the product of an accidental meeting at an
anti-nuclear meeting, represents the coming together of two very
different worlds, for which the "mental and geographical maps"
(38) overlap only incidentally. Edward and Florence are separated
by being from different backgrounds: he has never stayed in a
hotel before, while she has travelled extensively and is accus-
tomed to servants; his father Lionel is an overworked headmaster
in a country school, struggling to raise three children while caring for his wife, Marjorie, disabled by a brain injury; her mother
Violet is a philosophy professor and her father Geoffrey is a successful businessman with his own electronics factory. This class
divide is not an insurmountable obstacle, since Florence admires
Edward's intellect and education and her family quickly accepts
him. But more serious are their conflicting approaches to life; Florence is inclined to traditional social restraint, leading a staid and
disciplined life of rehearsals with her quartet, whereas Edward is
attracted to modern freedoms, including street violence, in which
he engages from time to time. This divergence, which is captured

in their musical tastes—classical for Florence, rock for Edward—is manageable until it becomes magnified by the issue of their unavoidable sexual encounter on their wedding night. The narrator wryly sums up their problem as one endemic to British culture at the time: "And what stood in their way? Their personalities and pasts, their ignorance and fear, timidity, squeamishness, lack of entitlement or experience or easy manners, then the tail end of a religious prohibition, their Englishness and class and history itself. Nothing much at all" (96).

The narratorial voice here and throughout *On Chesil Beach* conveys a sense of historical distance, a look back from our enlightened contemporary vantage point at a time when problems such as sexual inhibition were still difficult to speak about, though, as the narrator admits, "it is never easy" (3). This retrospective technique recalls, once again, *The French Lieutenant's Woman*, in which John Fowles's narrator, based in the sexually liberated late 1960s, peers through a metaphorical telescope at the lives of Charles Smithson and Sarah Woodruff a hundred years earlier, as they struggle against the Victorian boundaries of class and propriety that frustrate their desire for one another. Fowles's seaside setting of Lyme Regis, with its harbour wall The Cobb extending into the sea, along with the lovers' promontory in Matthew Arnold's "Dover Beach," is echoed in McEwan's choice of Chesil Beach as the locale for his characters' solitary confrontation. This remote 22-mile long spit, with its naturally graded pebbles (of which McEwan illegally took a few handfuls as souvenirs, causing a media storm until he returned them), and the couple's room in the nearby Georgian inn serve as isolated stages on which Florence and Edward play out their difficulties in talking freely about sex. On the *Out of the Book* DVD about *On Chesil Beach*, McEwan says that "it's as if they stand on a kind of shore, as it were, a beach, a beachhead of change."

Although both Edward and Florence are virgins, their knowledge of sexuality is vastly different, reflecting a persistent post-Victorian double-standard that kept women prudishly ignorant before marriage, but allowed men to share their experiences. While Edward has not had intercourse with anyone, he has an active sexual fantasy life, indulges frequently in masturbation, and seemingly has had one close encounter that ended badly because of "over-excitement," a condition which a male acquaintance described to him as "arriving too soon" (7). Edward at least has a euphemistic way of thinking about sexual activity, whereas Florence has no language in which to represent what she thinks of as a frightening social obligation, not the fulsome source of pleasure that Molly enjoys in *Amsterdam*. Florence is unable to discuss things with her sister, who is too young, or with her physically unaffectionate mother, who is "too intellectual, too brittle, an old-fashioned bluestocking" and resorts to "longer and longer words" (10) and references to obscure books when faced with an uncomfortable subject. Too reserved to approach her more uninhibited friends, Florence is left with only a "paperback guide," the cover of which is decorated with "two smiling bug-eyed matchstick figures holding hands, drawn clumsily in white chalk, as though by an innocent child" (11). Within this deceptively simple pamphlet is anatomical terminology that increases her sense of visceral revulsion—"mucous membrane," "glans," "engorged" (8)—and contributes to her tendency to see sexuality as a series of disconnected parts, something like the clippings from magazines that Marjorie Mayhew scatters around her home. As well, there are words in the guidebook that imply to Florence that she is to be treated as an object in a painful and humiliating way, to be forcibly "penetrated" and "entered" (9) as if she were a "portal or drawing room" (8). Beyond the obstacle of language, there is the subtle suggestion that she has been the victim of sexual abuse at the hands of her father, as she is beset by "memories she had long ago decided were not really hers" (105) of being alone with him on his boat, seeing him undressing, and feeling intense shame. Since "the language and practice of therapy ... were not yet in general circulation" (21), this crucial story remains repressed, as do both Florence and Edward's hidden fears about lovemaking.

On a number of levels, sex is figured in the novel both as a series of narratives that are difficult to convey in words and as acts of reading that fail to produce coherent meaning. Florence knows the language of music—"*legato, pizzicato, con brio*" (14)—and thinks in musical phrases, while Edward knows the names of wildflowers and birds; yet neither can articulate their basic anxieties about their intimate relationship, "to reveal themselves fully to one another" (6), both physically and emotionally. For the reader, privy equally to both of their thoughts in McEwan's highly expressive prose, their failure to find words in which to say what needs to be said is both poignant and frustrating. To Florence, her "condi-tion" is "unutterable" (7), "unnameable" (141), and "there existed no shared language in which two sane adults could describe such events to each other" (139). For his part, Edward relies on actions to communicate his wishes—the placement of his hand or hers, the thrusting of his tongue into her mouth—and before the wedding he interprets Florence's reactions to these gestures with some sophistication, slowing his advances when necessary. But in the hotel, overwhelmed by deferred desire and emboldened by his new married status, he loses his sensitivity to Florence's responses, grown more complex because of their changed circum-stances, so that he fails to notice that she feels suffocated by his probing kisses or that her leading him to the bed is an effort to escape from being confined.

Before the wedding, when Edward would occasionally "mis-read the signs" (90) there were opportunities for rectification; after it, though, misinterpretation is fatal, making a difficult situation worse. Tragically, he does not perceive when she becomes truly aroused for the first time as he massages her inner thigh and stim-ulates a stray pubic hair; knowing nothing about female arousal, he leaves off any further foreplay and moves directly to his own needs. In a scene redolent of Charles Smithson's seduction of Sarah Woodruff in Endicott's Hotel, Edward approaches her with his shirt still on, "covering his erection, like a draped public mon-ument" (98). This simile relating Edward's sexuality to military conquest calls attention to the aggressively masculine mindset he brings to what should be the mutual fulfillment of their desires. Her attention, on the other hand, is on how to "please him and make this night a success" (103), following the advice of the guide-book, which identifies male pleasure as the primary goal of con-summation. With both of them focused on him, the stage is set for disaster: she attempts to ease his entry by guiding his penis with her hand, bringing on his premature ejaculation and causing both of them to feel they have failed. Because they are unable to artic-ulate their feelings of shame, however, they interpret each other's reactions as disappointment and anger, especially Florence's open disgust at being coated in semen.

As in *Amsterdam*, the climactic moment leads to an irreparable breach. Florence's immediate response is to retreat to a secluded position out on the spit, in keeping with her behaviour in the past, for which her history of abuse may be responsible: "All these years she had lived in isolation within herself and, strangely, from herself, never wanting or daring to look back" (61). Edward, too, reverts to familiar ways of behaving, aggressively calling her a "bitch" (149), and then labeling her "frigid" (156) once she has finally found the courage to express her fear of sex and to propose that they have an open marriage that would allow them to maintain their love and satisfy his physical needs. Again, they are both guilty of poor interpretation of the other: Florence cannot perceive how her imagined scenario excludes a very important form of intimacy for him, and he believes he can represent her entire, complex problem with a single word. Unlike another seemingly "frigid" female character, Maude Bailey in A.S. Byatt's *Possession* (who also dislikes when the terminology of "entry" is used to describe intercourse), Florence is unable to convince her partner that a "modern way" (Byatt 550) is a viable possibility for their relationship. Only years later does Edward think of her proposal as "liberated," "far ahead of its time, innocently generous, an act of self-sacrifice that he had quite failed to understand" (160–1). They end up permanently separated, leading diminished lives, especially Edward, who never settles down in a marriage or a job, whereas Florence at least excels with her music. His final realization, "Love and patience—if only he had had them both at once—would surely have seen them both through" (166), suggests a solution that might have worked in their textual world, which has a potential for redemption that Clive and Vernon's intrinsically lacks.

While the socially repressive environment of *On Chesil Beach* may seem more remote to us than the libertine late capitalist world of *Amsterdam*, the former offers a model for compassionate treatment of others still relevant to our contemporary situation. As Violet Ponting explains, the problems of the past come back in different forms: the Apocalypse dreamed of in the Book of Revelation returns as the threat of nuclear war, and, we can extrapolate, the "medieval cults and wild, psychotic leaders" (44) studied by Edward reappear as terrorists and their training camps. Both of these short novels present dramatic conflicts between individuals that reflect on the moral blind spots of their times—greed, ambition, egotism, gender inequality—all of which are products of a concentration on the self to the detriment of others. Even

Clive, moved by Molly's gentle acceptance of Garmony's pecca-dilloes, comes to this realization: "We know so little about each other. We lie mostly submerged, like ice floes, with our visible social selves projecting only cool and white" (71). This perception, like Edward's belated understanding of Florence, opens the way to more a more benevolent society in any period.

8

ATONEMENT

"There were horrors enough, but it was the unexpected detail that threw him and afterwards would not let him go" (*Atonement* 191). This is the opening sentence of Part Two of McEwan's best-selling novel *Atonement*, the section in which Corporal Robbie Turner's grueling experiences during the retreat to Dunkirk are recounted. But it also captures my response to McEwan's treatment of war in the text: despite the convincing depictions of violence and suffering in Parts Two and Three, the latter dealing with Briony Tallis' wartime service as a nurse in a London hospital, I was frequently struck by "unexpected details" that suggested that McEwan's agenda in including these scenes went well beyond an urge to depict the Second World War in a historically realistic way. Notwithstanding the author's careful acknowledgement of historical source material, including soldiers' and nurses' reminiscences, the portions of the novel set during the War have distinct elements of literary fantasy and self-conscious construction. These graphic sections are oddly shot through with seemingly extraneous details repeated from Part One, which relates the events of one day on the Tallis estate in 1935, when the adolescent Briony persuades her visiting cousins to perform in a melodrama she has written; the emphasis on theatrical production in the opening underscores the artificially dream-like repetitions that pervade the novel from beginning to end, moving across a number of narrative levels.

One could argue that the novel's openly repetitive, or more accurately, recursive structure recasts events from the War in fantasy terms not to dilute their historical significance, but rather to point to the complexities of post-realist representation. As

Linda Hutcheon suggests in *A Poetics of Postmodernism,* such self-conscious textual gestures illuminate "the particular nature of the historical referent" (89), which exceeds containment by any discursive form. In this case, the overt fictiveness of McEwan's passages about the War could be seen as purposely drawing attention to the inherent impossibility of truly representing historical reality.

In an interview with Jonathan Noakes and Margaret Reynolds, McEwan acknowledges the centrality of self-conscious fiction-making to his conception of *Atonement.* While noting that Briony, the novel's main character, is modeled partly on *Northanger Abbey*'s Catherine Morland, "a girl so full of the delights of Gothic fiction that she causes havoc around her when she imagines a perfectly innocent man to be capable of the most terrible things" (20), McEwan explains that "part of the intention of *Atonement* was to look at story-telling itself. And to examine the relationship between what is imagined and what is true" (19). McEwan uses Briony's role as an imaginative teller of tales, established at the outset of Part One with her adolescent authorship of the melodrama *The Trials of Arabella,* as an internal reflection on the act of storytelling in general while creating a compelling narrative of his own; he admits, "I'm always drawn to some kind of balance between a fiction that is self-reflective on its own processes, and one that has a forward impetus, too, that will completely accept the given terms of the illusion of fiction" (20).

Yet there are clues throughout *Atonement* that such self-conscious fictionalizing can result in a denial of truth in favour of the projection of willful self-delusion. In the text's key moral encounter, Briony accuses Robbie, the son of Grace Turner, the estate's charwoman, of raping her cousin Lola Quincey, despite the ambiguity of the evidence, including Lola's own lack of corroboration. This false claim, brought on by Briony's exaggerated sense of her own interpretive powers as a neophyte author and her jealous oedipal attraction to older men including Robbie and her brother Leon, creates the disastrous consequences for Robbie, including imprisonment and ultimately death, that lead her to seek atonement—or "at-one-ment," "a reconciliation with the *self,*" as McEwan put it in an interview (qtd. in Schemberg 8n.)— through writing. Yet the tendency of Briony's written narratives towards self-aggrandizement and fantasy resolution rather than true reparation to others suggests that her egotism permeates all aspects of the text. Judith Seaboyer notes that

> the question becomes whether Briony's *Atonement* (sic) is simply an act of bad faith, or an act of love, or both, and whether the victims of her crime would have countenanced her efforts. From this perspective, Briony's use of an effaced third-person narration and free indirect discourse are problematised. Her desire to atone is complicated by her desire to arouse in us desire for her narrative. (2005: 32)

McEwan thus places the onus on the reader to see beyond the elaborate literary deception of his novel to the ethical position of genuine compassion for the other only apparently represented by his narcissistic main character.

A crucial moment in the plot of *Atonement* relies on the rather hackneyed device of the Freudian slip, in which repressed desire forces its way into language. After musing quite self-consciously about Freud's theories, Robbie mistakenly sends to Briony's sister Cecilia Tallis the erotic version of his letter to her rather than the chaster one he intended, setting into motion the events that lead to Briony's false condemnation of him and her consequent need to atone for her lie through writing. In her third-person narrative that makes up Part One of the novel, Briony figures herself in the scene in which the letter is transmitted as silent and spectral, a "white shape" (93) whose supernatural presence represents the released desire that has sprung up in textual form. It is tempting to read this crucial passage as a foundational trauma, whose effect ripples forward throughout the text as a series of repetitions. Yet as Slavoj Žižek suggests in "The Truth Arises from Misrecognition", the "synchronic" (189) nature of signification, including both the transferential narrative of psychoanalysis and fiction, plays havoc with conventional notions of temporality. In fact, he argues that the source of traumatic eruptions of desire such as Robbie's Freudian slip does not lie in the past: "The Lacanian answer to the question, from where does the repressed return, is then paradoxically: from the future. Symptoms are meaningless traces; their meaning is not discovered, excavated from the hidden depth of the past, but constructed retroactively" (188–9). Individual scenes or details from the text should therefore be seen as signs of "what will have been (*auront été*)" ("Truth" 189), the significance of which will only be evident in retrospect. This reversal of the diachronic accrual of meaning is intensified in *Atonement* by Briony's retroactive authority over the whole text, which though hinted at in Part One, is revealed fully only in the final section, headed "London, 1999."

But it is not enough to interpret the novel, with its repeated details and traumatic scenes, backward from the point of Briony's authorial revelation; one must take into account the varying levels of narration that come into play, creating a Chinese-box effect that progressively complicates the text's representational status. Although Part One reads initially as a third-person account of Briony's formative experiences as a writer at the age of 13, in the light of the final section it appears to be thinly disguised autobiographical fiction, establishing the real-life circumstances behind the wartime events in Parts Two and Three, up to Robbie and Cecilia's successful reunion in London. Yet the truth-claim of the novel's middle sections is obliterated by Briony's final admissions that both Robbie and Cecilia were killed during the war, casting doubt on the factual basis of anything she has written, including Part One, which implies that all of her characters, even Robbie and Cecilia, could be as fictitious as the dramatis personae in her play. This multi-layered, or recursive, structure is signalled by Briony's seemingly inexplicable notation on her writing-pad early on in the text, "There was an old lady who swallowed a fly" (115), the first line of a children's rhyme with a repetitive yet expanding pattern, terminating in the old lady's death. Psychoanalytic theorist Donald Spence discusses how recursive tales create a textual field similar to the manifest content in a dream, with the repetitive elements acting as signs of a "latent wish" (190). Within such a text, apparently identical repetitions also become variations based on their placement in a "spiral pattern" (193) of self-enclosing narratives. Every turn in the spiral, he suggests, necessitates a "shift in mode of representation" (202), so that with each telling, "the narrative voice keeps moving farther and farther into the fantastic and away from the conventional bounds of time and space" (188). In some cases, for instance Mary Shelley's *Frankenstein*, the spiral works its way back up through the embedded narrations to the original teller, restoring representational stability. In the case of *Atonement*, however, the ultimate establishment of Briony's authorship radically undermines the entire text's pretence to realism.

In fact, Part One contains many clues that the realistic ground beneath the feet of Parts Two and Three is shaky indeed. From the opening pages where Briony's childhood dramaturgical ambitions are inscribed, there is a pronounced sense of theatricality, such that all of the events seem staged and are watched through various framing devices—window frames, skylights, mirrors and so on—and often from a height, as if from a director's or camera-operator's point of view. Furthermore, a number of scenes are shown to be open to different interpretations, many of them false, such as Briony's mistaking in the dark the shape of the would-be rapist (actually Leon's friend and Lola's eventual husband, Paul Marshall) for a moving bush. This visual confusion contributes to Briony's indictment of Robbie, as she trusts her literary instincts more than sensory data: "It was not simply that her eyes that told her the truth. It was too dark for that . . . . Her eyes confirmed the sum of all she knew and had recently experienced . . . . It was her story, the one that was writing itself around her" (169, 166). Similarly, when Briony stumbles upon Cecilia and Robbie having sex in the library, she immediately jumps to the conclusion that an assault is underway, since she has read and been shocked by the erotic letter: "what she saw must have been shaped in part by what she already knew, or believed she knew" (123). The reader views this scene through young Briony's eyes first, but is already aware of Robbie's amorous feelings for Cecilia and is therefore unlikely to be swayed by Briony's lurid and rather naïve interpretation of the event as rape; the narrator's unfocalized description of the scene (still emanating, of course, from Briony's pen) some ten pages later should merely confirm the reader's assumptions. Conversely, a prior scene in which Briony watches from a window as Cecilia and Robbie struggle over a vase at the fountain is related first from the general narrator's point of view and then from Briony's sensational one, which is channeled, as always, through her self-absorbed focus on her development as a writer. Witnessing this "dumb show" (41) leads her to conclude that her writing thus far has been in the "wrong genre" (45) and that she must shift to a form of intense psychological realism that could encompass the complexities of adult life: "for her now it could no longer be fairy-tale castles and princesses, but the strangeness of the here and now, of what passed between people" (39).

This kind of generic anxiety haunts the first part of the novel, with Robbie agonizing over the most fitting style for his love letter to Cecilia; but it also takes the form of a veritable traffic-jam of intertextual influences on McEwan's part, from the Gothic elements introduced by the epigraph from *Northanger Abbey* to references to myths and fairy tales, as well as dramatic romances, comedies, tragedies and melodramas. All of this intense literary self-consciousness underscores Part One's deliberate staging of the aesthetic and cultural moment of modernity. Poised between the end of the First World War—which enjoys a kind mythic status in the text thanks to the heroics of the Tallis family uncle who carried the vase, later broken by Cecilia, safely through the trenches—and the onset of the Second World War, Part One plays isolation and timelessness against the imminent cataclysm that will form the basis of late twentieth-century contemporary reality. The Tallis estate, with its island temple and reproduction of Bernini's *Triton*, not to mention the Keatsian vase, seems on that day in 1935 to be outside time, regulated only by the daily rituals sensed by the mother Emily Tallis in her sickbed. Yet signs of change are everywhere: despite the pony-trap still driven by the servant Hardman, who considers himself "too old to learn to drive a car" (45) and the paintings of portraits of *faux* Victorian ancestors hanging in the dining hall, modernism hangs over the scene like a "Fauvist" (78) landscape.

Along with the modernist social revolution hinted at by Cecilia's admission to Oxford and Paul Marshall's *nouveau riche* class mobility comes a shift in the role of language. At first, Briony believes fervently in the traditional representational power of words; she muses, "Reading a sentence and understanding it were the same thing . . . . There was no gap during which the symbols were unravelled. You saw the word *castle*, and it was there" (37). The entrepreneur Marshall's arrival ushers in a more modern linguistic understanding; his Amo chocolate bars form part of a system of commercial naming, along with "Oxo and Brillo" (62), which assumes only a superficial correspondence between words and the things they represent. Like the skywritten advertisement at the beginning of *Mrs Dalloway* (an intertext reinforced by the oppressive heat in Part One of *Atonement*, along with Elizabeth Bowen's *The Heat of the Day*), language in McEwan's text verges on the sublime; he has the twins, Jackson and Pierrot, terrified by the unimaginable rupture signified by the word "divorce" (57), while Briony sees the word "cunt" in Robbie's letter to Cecilia as an endlessly fascinating object, which she reshapes into anagrams and rhymes (114). Lola's word for Robbie, "maniac," in Briony's mind "stir[s] the dust of other words around it—man, mad, axe, attack, accuse" (158) in a syntagmatic chain of signifiers.

In Part One, McEwan reflects upon language's separate materiality, its arbitrary (in the terms of Saussurian linguistics) relationship with the world it represents, from a conspicuously postmodern point of view; in fact, several of the characters experience an eerie sense of belatedness, as if they are aware of "what will have been." About Cecilia, for instance, the narrator notes, "All day long ... she had been feeling strange, and seeing strangely, as though everything was already long in the past, made more vivid by posthumous ironies she could not quite grasp" (48). This kind of hyperreal contemporary awareness makes the first section of *Atonement* seem as if it is "only a dream" (44), as Cecilia used to comfort her little sister after nightmares, a fabrication from which one can escape at will.

Following the radical destabilization of reality in Part One, the Dunkirk section announces itself in several ways as a kind of dream-text in which the manifest content conceals the existence of an underlying set of drives, most obviously Briony's need to atone, but also McEwan's desire to probe the complexities of contemporary representation. Slavoj Zizek notes how, in dreams, signifiers are only obliquely related to their signifieds; words and symbols function like "rebuses", such that "things literally *stand for their names*" ("Two Ways" 51), reminiscent of the reified, commercial language in Part One. In order to make sense of the dream-text, Zizek says, one must therefore treat it the way a detective approaches a staged crime scene: "The scene's organic, natural quality is a lure, and the detective's task is to denature it first by discovering the inconspicuous details that stick out" (53). The narrator does not attempt to conceal the hallucinatory nature of Robbie's experiences along the road to Dunkirk, though there is the suggestion that any oneiric confusion is in keeping with the psychological horror of the retreat. Yet throughout Part Two, for no apparent reason, details from Part One are repeated in slightly modified ways, continuing a pattern of repetition-with-variation established early in the novel with Jackson and Pierrot, who are identical except for a missing "triangle of flesh" (11) on one of the twins' ear because of a dog-bite.

These variable repetitions—which, as I noted earlier, contribute to the recursive distancing of text from the outside world—begin right away with Robbie's sighting of a severed child's leg up in a tree. This traumatic event recalls the near-tragedy in Part One of the twins' disappearance, averted by Robbie's heroic rescue of them, but it is also oddly prepared for by Briony's glimpse on that fateful evening of her mothers seemingly "disembodied" (161) leg, which is merely poised at a curious angle inside the window frame.

Other repetitions are closer to Žižek's theory of the rebus: for instance, the name of Corporal Nettle, one of the two enlisted men accompanying Robbie on the retreat, literally stands for the nettles that young Briony flays while daydreaming, a game she builds into her mind into an Olympic sport at which she is the champion. In writing Robbie's story, she turns the word associated with the memory into one half of a conventional comic duo; like Beckett's Gigi and Dodo in *Waiting for Godot* or the gravediggers in *Hamlet*, Nettle and Mace are almost interchangeable, and lend an air of slapstick to Robbie's desperate circumstances. Just as the heroic brother Leon scoops up the ravaged Lola in Part One and carries her to safety, Mace saves a puny, myopic RAF officer from an angry mob on the beach, racing him from the scene with perfect comic timing, "like Johnny Weissmuller's Tarzan" (253). Robbie thinks of him as "that brave bear, Corporal Mace" (263), casting him in fantastic terms something like the two-headed monster that Robbie himself is perceived to be when he arrives back at the estate with one of the missing twins atop his shoulder.

There are other points at which the Dunkirk section veers towards the mythological: in the coastal French town Robbie and Nettle meet a gypsy whom Robbie thinks somehow clairvoyantly knows his criminal past. Rather than simply taking from her what they want, Robbie agrees to capture her escaped pig in exchange for food and drink; with this act of "magical thinking," he believes he will ensure his safe passage home. This bizarre scenario, redolent of Odysseus's encounter with Circe, brings together from Part One both Grace Turner's cottage-industry fortune-telling and Betty the cook, who steams witch-like over her cauldron of food while putting aside scraps for her "Gloucester Old Spot, fattening for December" (104). As with the arrangement with the gypsy, practically all of Robbie's experiences in Part Two turn out happily; while a Flemish mother and her son are obliterated by a bomb attack, there is also the Brueghel-like farmer standing, perfectly unharmed, under a nearby tree with his dog, ready to resume his plowing. At the same time, Robbie dreams of escaping into the surrounding forest: "the woods were near, there would be streams and waterfalls and lakes in there. He imagined a paradise" (238). This fairy-tale impulse connects to the comic, essentially erotic, narrative straight from *The Trials of Arabella*, that underlies all of Part Two: the fantasized reunion between Robbie and Cecilia, their "Wiltshire dream" (208) of a cottage with the children all tucked safely into bed, as Robbie longs to do for the dead French boy with the severed leg.

Generically, then, the Dunkirk section of the novel avoids historical realism; rather, it presents a world in which, despite visceral horror, all turns out for the best, much like Leon's optimistic attitude: "In Leon's life, or rather, in his account of life, no one was mean-spirited, no one schemed or lied or betrayed . . . . The effect of one of Leon's anecdotes was to make his listener warm to humankind and its failings" (107). This inclination towards fantasy is heightened in Part Three, in which Briony attempts to compensate for her harmful actions towards Robbie by immersing herself in the "elated, generalized love" (305) of helping others. While the suffering in the London hospital scenes is every bit as gruesome as that in the Dunkirk section, there is still the curious tendency towards romantic resolution. Depicting herself as a modern version of that great Victorian heroine, Florence Nightingale (echoed earlier in the novel by the stories about the family's intrepid Auntie Venus, a nurse who survived the wilds of northern Canada), Briony gives comfort to the maimed and dying, while secretly keeping up her writing late at night. During one of her rare breaks from self-sacrifice, she attends the wedding of Paul Marshall and Lola Quincey, where she resists the temptation to disrupt the ceremony with the news that Marshall was indeed the rapist, not Robbie; instead, she represses the ugly reality in favour of the "formal neatness of virtue rewarded" (9) that a wedding represents, just as she would have done in her childhood plays.

Finally, in Part Three there is the poignant reunion of Robbie and Cecilia, and Briony's promise to publicly admit her false accusation. It is significant that this fantasized resolution takes place away from central London, in the suburbs where Briony goes to attend Lola's wedding to her supposed real assailant, Paul Marshall. Briony's journey away from the London hospital where she works as a nurse tending to grievously wounded men is framed as trip back to the timelessness of the novel's opening scene: Briony has only a "crumbling bus route map dated 1926" (318) to consult for directions, all the street signs and destination boards having been taken down to confuse German infiltrators; and the military demand for vehicles has led to cars being replaced with horses driven by contented milkmen, so that the suburban environment has a rustic air of long-ago innocence. Following her sentimental reflection on the "unthinking family love" (349) symbolized by her sister and Robbie's willingness to accept the sincerity of her remorse, Briony's authorship is established by the notation "London 1999" (349) and her initials, such that the fictional nature of the wartime narratives is at last made clear.

With the shift to the final layer of the Chinese-box and the contemporary first-person voice of Briony as a mature woman that underpins the rest of the text, it might be expected that a hitherto repressed sense of realism would come to the fore. After all, Briony has performed her work of atonement through writing and should no longer need to shape events artificially to convert tragedy into joy. In the final section, there is a new attention to historical truth: the now-famous author Briony relishes her correspondence with the real Corporal Nettle, who has helped her correct inaccuracies in her wartime narratives; and she longs to publish the novel that she has been writing over the course of 59 years, in which she exposes her crime as well as the complicity of Paul and Lola Marshall, now Lord and Lady. In that publication, she tells us, she would "disguise nothing—the names, the places, the exact circumstances—I put it all there as a matter of historical record" (369). At the same time, though, she admits to having produced at least eight drafts of this document—the first in 1940, the last in 1999 and a "half a dozen" (369) in between, all of them different—putting into question how historically accurate any of them is, and prompting the reader to wonder just which draft we have read as Part One. Still, Briony claims she is prevented from setting the record straight by the legal power of the Marshalls, and by her own vascular dementia, which is sapping her memory and hastening her death. She does, however, disclose to the reader the "true" fates of Robbie and Cecilia, both of whom died in 1940 without ever having been reunited.

Yet even these gestures towards truth-telling and realism are short-lived. That tragic outcome does not accord with Briony's "wish for a harmonious, organized world" (5), so instead she changes the genre of her story about Robbie and Cecilia something closer to a comedy:

> How could that constitute an ending? What sense of hope or satisfaction could a reader draw from such an account? Who would want to believe that they never met again, never fulfilled their love? Who would want to believe that, except in the service of bleakest realism? .... I know there's always a certain kind of reader who will be compelled to ask, But what *really* happened? The answer is simple: the lovers survive and flourish. As long as there is a single copy, a solitary typescript of my final draft, then my spontaneous, fortuitous sister and her medical prince survive to love. (371)

While Briony tries to justify this distortion as not "weakness or evasion, but a final act of kindness" (372) by an old woman towards the long-dead couple, the artificial reinstatement of the happy ending recalls her youthful attraction to order, which is carried over into her writing: "Only when a story was finished, all fates resolved and the whole matter sealed off at both ends so it resembled, at least in this one respect, every other finished story in the world, could she feel immune ...." (6).

The immunity that the adolescent Briony seeks here is from "self-exposure" (6), the revelation of her own ego through her work, which she fears is inevitably seen by her readers as a reflection of herself rather than a true imaginative creation of the other. She muses on the separate lives of other people: "was everyone else really as alive as she was? For example, did her sister really matter to herself, was she just as valuable to herself as Briony was?" (36). In interviews, McEwan has cited this curiosity of Briony's as the model of "precisely that quality of fiction writing that most appeals to [him]: that sense of being able to give the reader what it means to be someone else" (Eberhart). This ability to enter deeply into the mind of another, he believes, "lies at the foundation of our morality" (Eberhart). For Briony, though, the prospect that every-one else's inner life is as vivid as hers is disturbing, making the world "unbearably complicated" and threatening her as an individual with "irrelevance" (36). She would prefer, it seems, to be "surrounded by machines, intelligent and pleasant enough on the outside, but lacking the bright and private *inside* feeling she had" (36). While she knows that others must have a sense of interiority similar to her own, she does so "only in a rather arid way; she didn't really feel it" (36).

As we have seen, the first part of the novel establishes that Briony suffers from an inflated sense of her own creative genius and a tendency to let her desires influence her understanding of events. She believes that, as a novelist, she possesses a kind of "absolute power of deciding outcomes" that makes her like "God" (371). Her demonstration of her power is clear in the reshaping of her wartime narratives into fantasy texts that suppress the harsh reality of her crime and its aftermath. This generic manipulation culminates in the final section, in which Briony, despite her serious medical condition, enjoys her own happy ending in the form of a loving reunion with her family and a successful performance of *The Trials of Arabella*. The Marshalls, who coincidentally cross her path on this fateful day, appear finally only as impotent cartoonish villains, with Lola as an aged "Cruella de Vil" (358).

In *Achieving "At-one-ment": Storytelling and the Concept of the Self in Ian McEwan's* The Child in Time, Black Dogs, Enduring Love, and Atonement, Claudia Schemberg argues that, by the end of her narrative, Briony has made a legitimate effort to transcend her narcissism: while "Briony's youthful imagination ruthlessly and ego-istically subordinated the world and other people to schemes and patterns . . . such as fairy-tales," her more mature artistic concep-tion, evident in the sections of the text relating Robbie and Cecilia's experiences during the Second World War and her own final days in 1999, "furnishes a final proof that in her quest for atonement Briony has learned how to imaginatively put herself in the posi-tion of other people" (85). Schemberg locates this compassionate response in Briony's refusal to fabricate Robbie's forgiveness for her role in his incarceration and death in the war. Certainly, Briony could have added an emotional scene of complete reconciliation to her narrative; but she notes that she "was not so self-serving as to let them forgive [her]" (372). In her god-like role as author, she feels that there is "no entity or higher form that she can appeal to, or be reconciled with, or that can forgive her" (371); her refusal to manufacture absolution through her characters can therefore be seen as part of her self-imposed penance.

There is, of course, another "entity or higher form" to which Briony is subtly appealing here: the reader, who can choose to believe that her act of atonement has been a genuine one. Certainly, Briony's popularity as a character and the generally positive treatment she has received at reviewers' hands would suggest that many readers, like Schemberg, are willing to accept her sincerity. But to do so fully, we must consider a number of questions. If her intention is to recreate faithfully the lost lives of those she has harmed, why does she imbue the various layers of her narrative with such stylized repetitions and self-conscious elements of fantasy and literary romance? Why, after the realistic suffering of the wartime passages, does she recast her characters in the final section as stock figures from a melodrama, pleasant machines rather than the sorts of complex psychological beings she imagined herself writing about as a child? And why does she end her account as she began it, in such a self-centered fashion with her triumphant career as a writer at center-stage? McEwan leaves his readers many clues that Briony's remorse may be only skin deep; the true complexity of this novel lies in discovering the ethical deficit of its main character, whose "at-one-ment" or reconciliation is with the self, but not the other.

9

SATURDAY

Looking out over London early one morning, Henry Perowne, the main character in *Saturday*, thinks that "the city is a success, a brilliant invention, a biological masterpiece—millions teeming around the accumulated and layered achievements of the centuries, as though around a coral reef, sleeping, working, entertaining themselves, harmonious for the most part, nearly everyone wanting it to work" (5). This positive view of contemporary urban life is reinforced by the epigraph from *Herzog*, in which Saul Bellow's character celebrates the city as a kind of "beautiful supermachinery opening a new life for innumerable mankind" (n.p.). Herzog's image, like Perowne's, is reminiscent of Le Corbusier's modernist vision of a "radiant city," intended to serve as the answer to the question: "What kind of a life should a machine age man really lead?" (*Radiant City*, 105). Certainly, with its praise of the vast technological resources of modern urban living, from traffic circulation to humble inventions such as the electric tea kettle, McEwan's rendition of contemporary London life, conveyed by a third-person narrator but virtually exclusively focalized through Perowne's privileged perspective, verges on the utopian.

Yet McEwan's ideal city, like Bellow's, is undermined by the very forces of modernity that made it possible: "Subject to tremendous controls. In a condition caused by mechanization. After the late failure of radical hopes" (n.p.). As we have seen in the discussions of novels such as *The Comfort of Strangers* and *The Innocent*, a recurring feature of McEwan's urban fiction is the reification of various structures of power—inequality, state authority, military might, Western hegemony and capitalist dominance—in the representation of the city spaces, both internal and external. As Henri Lefebvre contends in *The Production of Space*, the city is always already "the setting of struggle" (386), with violence concealed beneath the surface of bourgeois activity. In *The Body and the City*, Steve Pile glosses Lefebvre's psychoanalytic argument, suggesting that "the urban fabric 'suffers' from emotional intensity: whether it is expressed in street violence, in the investments in monumental space or in the homes of the moneyed classes" (215). This seemingly incongruous trio of sites, where the repressed violence of city life becomes manifest —the street, monuments and middle-class houses—is central to the conception of London in McEwan's latest novel.

In *Saturday*, some of this underlying violence takes the form of the city's indigent and criminal individuals, "people [who] remember their essential needs and how they're not being met" (61). Frequently and conspicuously, the focalized narrative openly identifies these trouble-makers, along with other minor characters, according to their racial or cultural derivations, such as the three Muslim women in "black burkhas" who "have a farcical appearance, like kids larking about at Halloween" (124). Despite such overt racial coding, as Elizabeth Kowaleski Wallace points out, the cityscape in the novel is "mostly devoid of London's vibrant multicultural scene" (465), a postcolonial urban reality that Perowne selectively filters out and with which he only engages intermittently at the level of surface identification as people and events intrude into his otherwise imperturbable middle-class consciousness.

In the context of the narration's superficial sensitivity to cultural identities, the race of the text's main villain, the thug Baxter who terrorizes first the neurosurgeon Perowne and then his entire family, seems oddly to have been left deliberately vague; yet it is apparent that Baxter, and the domestic menace he represents, parallels the looming international threat of Islamist militantism, as demonstrated by the 9/11 attacks that serve as the novel's historical backdrop, and which the imminent invasion of Iraq in the text is ostensibly meant to contain. What is fascinating about *Saturday* is how completely and by what means the internal danger—and by implication, perhaps, the external one as well—is neutralized. Wallace notes that Baxter is so "one-dimensional" and powerless that "if indeed he stands in for a larger and more persistent menace—the militant poor, the citizens of the developing world, or even an Arab extremist—then McEwan's fantasy becomes especially facile" (476). Perowne's brutal encounter with Baxter inside his home, like everything else about his perambulation around London, establishes his ultimate sense of mastery over all that is disorderly, irrational and counter to the city's middle-class prosperity. This power to subdue the threatening other is clearly associated by McEwan (ironically or otherwise) with an attitude of British nationalism and imperialism reified in aesthetic terms by both art and the sublime beauty of the city itself.

With his multiple physical and intellectual endowments, Perowne is the obvious embodiment of this imperial authority. As a white, well-educated Englishman, he is reaping the benefits of privatized medical care in the post-Thatcher era through his successful neurosurgical practice; in him, Lee Siegel suggest, McEwan has "captured an essential quality of the bourgeois, consumerist West" (34). Perowne openly acknowledges his "egotistical joy in his own skills" and thinks of himself as being "like a god, an angel" (23) when he delivers a patient from mortal danger. The members of his family are equally gifted: his wife Rosalind is a lawyer valiantly fighting for the freedom of the tabloid press; his son Theo is a self-taught blues musician, encouraged by some of the art-form's greats; his daughter Daisy is an award-winning poet, publishing her first book of poems in her early twenties with a major press; even his mother, Lily, was a champion swimmer. Perowne himself, tall and fit, has a powerful physical presence, which he exerts in his athletic competitions with colleagues, whom he dominates both at work and outside. He presides as freehold landlord over his opulent townhouse in London, a legacy from Rosalind's mother, which is complemented with a literal castle in France, also hereditary, over which he intends to claim proprietorship following the death of his father-in-law, the famous poet John Grammaticus. While the properties are inherited, his car, a silver Mercedes, is a visible sign of his own power of acquisition, and he drives it with a sense of competence and entitlement, tinged with the "gentle, swooning joy of possession" (76).

With its liberating effects, the car serves as tangible proof to Perowne of the progressive character of contemporary life, epitomized by his culture's technological and scientific advances. He cites the views of two prominent scientists: Charles Darwin's reflection on evolution, "*There is grandeur in this view of life*" (55, italics in original) and a line from Peter Medawar, the 1960 Nobel laureate in medicine, "To deride the hopes of progress is the ultimate fatuity" (77). Despite his fears about the new dangers of post-9/11 existence, Perowne is convinced that Western progress itself will act as a shield against attacks by what he sees as less sophisticated peoples, and that reason, which he values over imagination, will prevail over religious fanaticism.

From his first appearance in the text, Perowne is associated with the Enlightenment values of rationality and order. Looking out from the second-floor window, Perowne is impressed by the view below, "a triumph of congruent proportion; the perfect square laid out by Robert Adam enclosing a perfect circle of garden—an eighteenth-century dream bathed and embraced by modernity" (5). Yet this neo-classical vision of symmetry barely conceals a history of violence; Perowne reflects that the "Regency façade on the other side of the square . . . is a reconstruction, a pastiche— wartime Fitzrovia took some hits from the Luftwaffe" (4). That historical threat from the sky metamorphoses into its contemporary version, the 9/11 terrorists, in the form of the flaming plane that Perowne sees streaking across the London sky in the novel's opening, an image later refracted as the "flash of red" (81) that is Baxter's careening car. Although the fiery plane, despite Theo's direst predictions, lands safely and turns out to contain nothing more threatening—or less decadently Western—than child pornography smugglers, its intrusion into Perowne's morning temporarily disrupts his orderly and secure conception of the world.

Similarly, the background presence of a local monument— the British Telecom Tower, or Post Office Tower, as it is called in the novel—serves to signify yet conceal the subcurrent of violence in contemporary London society. Perowne notices the Tower from his window in the text's opening scene, sees it as "a valiant memorial to more optimistic days" (4). Beyond the structure's obvious association—as a "glass-paned stalk" (196)— with the World Trade Centre as the burning plane passes by, it symbolizes a history of British technological development in the Cold War. It was built in the 1960s as a central part of a massive telecommunications network, designed to survive a nuclear attack (its circular structure was based on buildings left standing in Hiroshima and Nagasaki). The Tower was of such key military importance that it was designated an "official secret" until the mid-1990s and left off ordnance survey maps (http://www.urban75.org/london/telecom.htm). It was nonetheless the target of a terrorist bombing attack in 1971.

According to Lefebvre, monuments play a number of key roles in the urban environment. They orient "walkers in the street," mirroring back to them "their place in the world, geographically, historically and socially" (Pile 213). But with their visual impression of verticality and phallic strength, they are "also thoroughly infused with power relations" (Pile 212). These power relations are, at the same time, oddly visible yet invisible; Lefebvre writes,

> Monumentality . . . always embodies and imposes a clearly intelligible message. It says what it wishes to say—yet it hides a good deal more: being political, military, and ultimately fascist in character, monumental buildings mask the will to power and the arbitrariness of power beneath signs and surfaces which claim to express collective will and thought. (143)

In other words, monuments "legitimate" or "naturalise" (Pile 213) power relations associated with violent history such that they can persist almost unnoticed in the modern city.

While surveying the city early on the morning of Saturday, February 15, 2003—also the day of London's massive protest against the imminent invasion of Iraq, both historically and in the text—Perowne is blessed with the precise, clear vision that is just one attribute of his power: he wooed his wife by assisting in the surgical recovery of her sight, and he later gains the upper hand over Baxter with a visual diagnosis of his Huntingdon's disease. When Perowne looks down from his superior position onto the square, he regards it as a kind of dramatic space—analogous to the surgical theatre where he wields absolute authority—in which various London citizens play out scenarios from their sordid lives. These vignettes Perowne watches with the "remote possessiveness of a god" (13), and frequently admires the aesthetic properties of the creation below him; he enjoys the "pigeon excrement hardened by distance and cold into something almost beautiful" (4–5) and the passage of two nurses, "hot little biological engines with bipedal skills suited to any terrain" (13).

In fact, thinks Perowne, "there's no shortage of happiness" (61) among the visitors to the square, that microcosm of the city at large, and he likes to imagine himself as being like "Saddam, surveying the crowd with satisfaction from some Baghdad ministry balcony" (62). The apparent irony behind this simile is underscored by the revelation immediately following it of Perowne's practically unequivocal support for the upcoming invasion of Iraq, justified by his knowledge of the sheer unhappiness of the people under Saddam's balcony, as made known to him by an Iraqi patient. Another layer of complexity in the Perowne-as-Saddam comparison lies in the character's historical namesake, the diplomat Stewart Henry Perowne, who was stationed in the Middle East during and after the Second World War, helping to solidify British imperial interests in the region. Henry Perowne, in his pose as pseudo-beneficent ruler at the window, conveys some of that attitude of British colonialism, particularly towards the poor and non-white, whom he judges with Hussein-like cold-heartedness. For instance, he observes a young woman in an argument with her pusher-boyfriend, considers going out to offer her medical relief from her reaction to heroin, but then hesitates, looking at the extravagant "nineteenth-century French chandelier that hangs from the high ceiling" (65), and self-righteously abandons the girl to her fate.

The ethical burlesque of this scene, with McEwan's only seemingly ironic juxtaposition of the Saddam analogy and Perowne's opposition to the war, reveals the inherently imperious (and imperialist) cast of mind of the novel's main character. Perowne's thinking about his fellow Londoners is captured in Theo's song, "City Square," the lyrics for which begin, "*Baby, you can choose despair / Or you can be happy if you dare*" (170, italics in original). Happiness, for Perowne, is the product of choice, and the power to make that choice rests largely in people's willingness to be industrious. Towards the end of the novel, he "remember[s] the square at its best," with people "loll[ing] on the grass in quiet groups, men and women of various races, mostly in their twenties and thirties, confident, unoppressed, fit from private gym workouts, at home in their city" (272). What separates these fortunate souls from "the various broken figures that haunt the benches," he thinks, is work: "It can't just be class or opportunities—the drunks and junkies come from all kinds of backgrounds, as do the office people"

(272). History, race, class and social evolution play no part in Perowne's conception of urban life; like the members of his family, he believes, anyone can succeed brilliantly in London so long as they are hard-working. The exceptions to this comic vision are those unfortunate few who are genetically programmed to fail:

> Perowne, the professional reductionist, can't help thinking it's down to invisible molecules. It's a dim fate, to be the sort of person who can't earn a living, or resist another drink . . . . No amount of social justice will cure or disperse this enfeebled army haunting the public places of every town. (272)

The exemplar of this kind of genetic "bad luck" (272), of course, is Baxter, who comes to represent the unruly other whom Perowne must restrain for the sake of general order.

Superficially, it would seem that Baxter's condition—the incurable and horribly debilitating Huntingdon's disease—supports Perowne's belief that certain people, be they impoverished London street sweepers or prisoners in Abu Ghraib, are simply victims of ill fortune. Throughout the novel Perowne occasionally experiences a "vertiginous moment" (74) when he feels a deep connection with such people, and appreciates the basic interchangeability of human life. In his first confrontation with Baxter, Perowne, dressed like a "scarecrow" (86) in his squash attire, feels in fact as if he is just playing the role of the aggrieved middle-class man whose luxury car has been damaged in a fender-bender. Yet a deeper consideration of the scene suggests that there is nothing accidental about the conflict between these two characters, who represent two radically opposed facets of London society.

Baxter's initial appearance in the text is framed such that his difference, and indeed his inferiority, is highlighted. In the background of the encounter is the "unrelenting throb" (85) of the "tribal drums of the peace mongers" (87), who oppose Perowne's world view and therefore are another sign of savage disorder. Baxter and his cronies, Nark and Nigel, are consistently portrayed in animalistic terms: they look up "like deer disturbed in a forest" (84), Nigel is repeatedly referred to as "the horse-faced fellow" (85), and he turns over "the shorn-off wing mirror" of Baxter's car "the way one might a dead animal" (84). There are plenty of hints that Baxter and his gang are mixed up with the lowest elements of London's street culture: they wear "trainers, track-suits and hooded tops—the currency of the street, so general as to be no style at all" (5), and they speak in rapper slang. Perowne's run-in with them takes place after he has been granted the special privilege of crossing a closed-off street, likely in deference to his evident social status, and as the men are fleeing from a lap-dancing club. While Perowne acknowledges that lap-dancing is probably legal, he immediately associates the men with "criminality, drug-dealing" (83) based on the make of their car.

As I mentioned earlier, Baxter's race is unspecified, which is curious in the context of descriptions of minor characters such as the "much-loved Cockney lady who helps clean the theatres" (9), the "Filipino nurse" (105), not to mention that much-maligned Italian, the "feckless Giulio" (241) who has dared to impregnate Daisy. Baxter, instead, is characterized as merely sub-human, a flying monkey to Perowne's scarecrow:

> He's a fidgety, small-faced young man with thick eyebrows and dark brown hair razored close to the skull. The mouth is set bulbously, with the smoothly shaved shadow of a strong beard adding to the effect of a muzzle. The general simian air is compounded by sloping shoulders . . . . (87–8)

Perowne's first response to him is visceral repulsion, and he regrets not being "the machete-wielding type" (85) of surgeon, comfortable with wielding a blade. Yet, as he gains control over the situation by correctly diagnosing Baxter's medical condition, Perowne combines modern scientific mastery with atavism: "He has the impression of himself as a witch doctor delivering a curse" (94). At this point, Perowne leaves behind his rationalistic sense of certainty and embraces the magical, which he claims to disdain in all its manifestations, including fiction. In the process, he becomes, for a moment, more like Baxter, a transformation repeated in the scene of his competitive squash game with Jay Strauss, where he behaves in a primitive, furious manner much like that of his supposed inferior.

Unlike Baxter, though, who can only decline into madness, Perowne is able to engage with the irrational in ways that are always temporary and constructive, allowing him to re-establish his superiority over threatening elements. Despite misgivings that he may have exacerbated the encounter in the street with his attitude, which may have seemed "pompous" or "provocative" (112), Perowne feels that he was warranted in vanquishing Baxter with scientific knowledge, that he "was obliged, or forced to abuse his own power" (111), an assessment later seconded by Rosalind. His exoneration rests on the justifiability of self-defence in the dangerous world of contemporary London, where middle-class citizens such as him must protect themselves in their homes and in their vehicles with elaborate security systems. This justification of self-defensive action against a potential threat is clearly meant to parallel the arguments being mounted in the background of the text by Prime Minister Blair, who, in spite of his own fallibility and uncertainties, is urging his compatriots to carry out a preemptive strike on Iraq. Just as the protestors warn the Prime Minister of the fatal consequences of his decision, including terrorist retaliation, Theo cautions his father about the possible repercussions of "humiliat[ing]" (152) those less powerful than him. Theo's fears, born out of his experiences with people on the street and his love for paranoid Internet conspiracy theories, materialize in the family's final confrontation with Baxter, which, on one level, replays in miniature the domestic invasion of 9/11.

McEwan immediately establishes the domestic sphere in *Saturday* as being deeply imbricated within larger structures of contemporary social power. For Lefebvre, the bourgeois home is the "guarantor of meaning" in capitalist society because it enables the steady continuation of "production and reproduction" (232) through the self-perpetuating role of the heterosexual family. In this setting, sexual activity is generally confined to the bedroom of the heterosexual couple and the rest of the house devoted to "an atmosphere of family and conjugal life—in short, of genitality" (315). Despite the apparent conviviality of this arrangement, Lefebvre contends, the bourgeois home becomes a symbolic site of a "repressed erotic life" (Pile 215) that is submissive to the Law that mirrors the ordering of the city along lines of economic, cultural and political dominance. The home and the city are thus contiguous and interrelated spaces, both prone to the "emotional intensity" and violent expression that result from the suppression of various kinds of desire.

When Baxter invades Perowne's home, which is normally as impregnable as a castle, he brings the violent consequences of cultural domination into the bourgeois stronghold, and the struggle is played out in the coded spaces of that edifice. Gaston Bachelard calls the study of the symbolic importance of different parts of houses "topoanalysis": "the systematic psychological study of the sites of our intimate lives" (8). The Perowne home is subtly organized to reflect certain structures of power, both personal and political. The upper story, as we have seen, is associated with Perowne's class superiority and cultural imperialism; it is also the location of his study, with its store of medical information, and the bedroom where he enjoys sexual intimacy with his wife Rosalind, reflecting the genital and heterosexual centrality of the home described by Lefebvre. The basement, on the other hand, where the kitchen is located, is connected with the traditionally feminine work of preparing food, here taking the form of Perowne's celebrated fish stew, made ready for the reunion of Henry and Rosalind with their children and their maternal grandfather, John Grammaticus. The first floor of the home, the shared living area with its street-level access, is the middle space where masculine and feminine principles converge as the conflict between the bourgeois family and the outsider takes place.

In this situation where the repressed violence of the city threatens to destabilize the phallic order of the home, the apparent gender equality of Henry's relationship with Rosalind, and of his two children's equally impressive artistic careers, gives way to a situation where conventional roles of male dominance and female passivity prevail. The male family members, including the usually drunkenly obnoxious Grammaticus, act bravely in defense of the beleaguered women, while the dishonourable Nigel deserts his comrade for the second time that day. Although Daisy is forced to strip and menaced with rape—an apparent recasting of the humiliation of Iraqi prisoners by American soldiers—her pregnancy keeps her from any serious harm.

The ascendance of masculine power is paralleled by the elevation of English middle-class culture, as Baxter is "transfixed" by the "magic" (278) of Daisy's recitation of Matthew Arnold's 'Dover Beach', which he mistakes as her own composition; he finds the poem "beautiful," and it "makes [him] think about where [he] grew up" (222). Such transcendent moments are always related in the text to a sense of comic resolution, an aesthetically idealized vision of the world in which Western values, and particularly those associated with British culture, are reaffirmed and any aberrant influences negated. This connection between the extreme presentism of poetry, which "balances itself on the pinprick of the moment" (129), and nostalgia has its analogue in the dementia of Perowne's mother Lily, for whom the past and the present are indistinguishable. Theo's blues music, like the "magical realist" novels that McEwan rather ironically has Perowne dismiss as "irksome confections" (67), can also produce this effect of being transported outside existence to the timeless.

This ideological combination neutralizes the latent violence let loose in the street, setting the stage for Baxter's return to his debased and silenced social position by being symbolically hurled down the stairs from Perowne's study to suffer further brain injury. Yet the crucial scene with the Arnold text only partially conceals the real historical conflict so neatly disposed of in the Perownes' home. When he first hears the poem, the doctor, an incarnation of the Arnold's art-loathing "philistine", imagines "desert armies stand[ing] ready to fight" (221), a misinterpretation he disregards the second time through as anachronistic. The clear symbolic valance of Baxter as post-9/11 threat, however, makes him the anarchic other that can—and must—be civilized by Arnoldian culture. The fact that Baxter is so easily subdued by the blandishments of the English literary tradition, as well as by the genius of scientific rationalism, points to a dream of imperial mastery in the contemporary setting that is built, however ironically, into McEwan's narrative.

In fact, everything to do with the middle-class characters turns out well: Henry's initial seduction of Rosalind is "effortless," "his wish come true, not a finger lifted, the envy of gods and despots" (50); the silver Mercedes is magically undamaged; Schrödinger's cat (to use Perowne's analogy) is always alive. With the defeat of Baxter, the family glories in its accomplishments and joins together in loving companionship, with the hope of a bright future symbolized by Daisy's child. Perowne feels "he's a king, he's vast, accommodating, immune, he'll say yes to any plan that has kindness and warmth at its heart" (269). This benevolence extends to Baxter, whom Perowne mercifully wishes to release from criminal charges, which were naturally not even considered by the police against the family itself. By performing life-saving surgery on Baxter, the doctor believes that he has granted forgiveness both to himself and to his antagonist, who emerges from the operation as if reborn, with his head "cradl[ed]" (256) in Perowne's hands. Baxter's rebirth, of course, is only into a life of steady decline and poverty, a return to his own inexorable history, while Perowne, with his work, feels "he's been delivered into a pure present, free of the weight of the past or any anxieties about the future" (258).

This sense of privileged order is reified in *Saturday* as the city itself. The story is structured around Perowne's successful navigation around London, beginning and ending at home, with the doctor safely in bed with Rosalind, pre- and post-coitus. By patterning his hero after those famous urban travelers Leopold Bloom and Clarissa Dalloway, McEwan builds in an element of literary inevitability, which is unbroken, even by Perowne's scrapes with Baxter. Part of this journey involves a trip out into the suburbs to visit Lily in her care home, where she is trapped in her psychic prison of diminishing sanity; she repeatedly frets, "There's hardly enough space to squeeze through. There's too much binding" (162). This anxiety becomes associated in Lily's mind with a pastoral vision of freedom; she tells her son: "Out here it only looks like a garden, Aunty, but it's the countryside really and you can go for miles . . . . You'll squeeze through somehow" (167). Driving back into the city, Perowne is mesmerized by the beauty of in-bound traffic—"all this teeming illumination" (168)—then is uplifted even more by Theo's song to a point of absolute liberation: "And here it is now, a coherent world, everything fitting at last . . . . He knows what his mother meant. He can go for miles . . ." (172). With this sequence of images, McEwan recreates the city as an aestheticized site in which the strictures of modernist urbanity give way to a kind of utopian self-fulfillment made possible by contemporary life.

This ideal state is reflected in the reordering of the urban landscape once the exterior threat represented by Baxter has been eliminated. Baxter's female counterpart, Andrea, the trash-talking, street-wise Nigerian girl staying in Brixton who is also saved by Perowne's skills, ends the novel in a state of romantic docility. As Perowne is drifting off to sleep for the final time in the book, he imagines the multiracial denizens of the square peaceably chatting. Through the focalized narration, the serene order of the city also becomes abstracted into images that crystallize Perowne's ultimate supremacy: his surgery has "the ephemeral tranquility of a city just before dawn" (261), while Baxter's exposed brain is an idyllic landscape, "a kind of homeland, with its low hills and enfolded valleys," its problematic parts "like bad neighbourhoods in an American city" (254) that the doctor is skilled enough to avoid straying into.

In its final pages, *Saturday* seems to anticipate the 2005 terrorist attacks: London, thinks Perowne, is "impossible to defend, waiting for its bomb" (276). Despite the apparent prescience and verisimilitude of McEwan's text, the London represented within it exists in a parallel dimension where violence is always containable; it is a projection of British nationalistic power, a vision of contemporary Western urbanity that is both disturbingly and utterly fantastic. With London's bomb inevitably coming, we should come away from the novel with the sense that something crucial, something imminent and frightening is being concealed by Perowne's elegant world. Yet one gets no sense of a need for urgent cultural change from the novel's ending, which papers over the implications of the disparity between the doctor and the street-thug and suggests that life can go on happily for the English middle class. There is no direct indictment of Henry Perowne's vision of things, and if McEwan's famous irony is at play here, its subtlety has obviously been lost on readers and critics alike, who hail the book as a masterpiece of British fiction.

PART III

Criticism and Contexts

10

AUTHOR INTERVIEW

December 7, 2005

LW: The book I'm writing will be focusing on the issue of ethics, particularly ethical encounters between characters. When I started spending a lot of time with your work, something that really struck me was how often there are encounters between particularly two individuals that create a kind of ethical dilemma. But I'm also interested in representational issues, particularly around self-conscious textuality. The rest of my questions will come out of other interviews, things I've heard you talk about before and wanted to hear more of what you have to say about those particular issues.

My first question has to do with fiction as a kind of moral form. You've talked a lot in other interviews about how you see the novel as a medium that allows for compassionate understanding of the other. Do you think that in your more recent fiction your interest in the novel as a moral or ethical form has changed from your earlier work?

IM: I think it has certainly changed from the work I did in the 70s and early 80s. Then I was more interested in surfaces. I thought it was almost cheating to let the reader know what a character was thinking. It seemed antiquated, a dead aesthetic, to provide paragraph summaries of someone's state of mind: I thought a subjective state had to be conveyed through observed details or simply by what people said and did. Later this existential kind of writing came to seem very self-limiting, and my fiction began to change around the time of *The Child in Time*. What fiction does better than any other art form is represent consciousness, the flow of thought, to give an interior narrative, a subjective history of an individual through time, through every conceivable event, through love, crises or moral dilemmas. This inner quality is what I now value.

So, to answer your question, once you move inside a person, once you allow your reader direct access, then you are in a much more moral frame. As I've said before, empathy, knowing what it is to be someone else, is at the foundation of our moral sense. As for self-consciousness there was another shift in my writing after *Enduring Love*. With that novel I had come to the end of a series of four books whose first motives were ideas, exploratory premises. The next book, *Amsterdam*, grew out of character, feeling, the vaguest of hunches, no intellectual motives at all; oddly, this mild *jeu d'esprit* did free me to write *Atonement*.

LW: Can you explain that?

IM: Yes. Those novels, from *The Child in Time*, right through to *Enduring Love*, their first steps, their first movements came out of ideas about the world for which I was looking for a fictional form. They were in some sense novels of ideas—in my own view of them, anyway. And *Amsterdam* started without prescriptions, or controlling ideas, nothing. I discovered the value of stopping thinking. I began *Atonement* with a blank slate, with greater freedom. If it appears to be "inter-textual" or "self-referencing" that is only because my head is stuffed with the pleasures of reading. As for ethics perhaps the shift was from a moral system I wanted to impose to a moral world that becomes illuminated as the thing unfolds. That is probably a very confused answer. To repeat, the apprehension of other minds is something that we're cognitively sophisticated at doing, perhaps instinctually so. People who are unable to do it aren't able to function socially.

LW: Like terrorists? You've said in other interviews . . .

IM: Well, like terrorists, but also like autistic children, like psychopaths too. There's a deep pathology involved for people who are not able to read other people's faces and gestures, and to make meaningful interpretations of their intentions, states of mind and so on. In other words, it is a basic human quality, to have a sense of what someone else is like, a sense that they're fundamentally like you. And yes, by extension then, certain acts of cruelty become failures of imagination. And I believe this is the moral basis of the novel, in that ability, in the "reading" of character, and in the invention of character. Other minds—a difficult notion, I think, to comprehend as a small child, and coming to terms with it is, in part, what we call moral growth. It is the journey you make. Now and then, you confront someone who doesn't seem to have quite made that journey, or made only two-thirds of it. At the other extreme, there are people who make the journey to excess, who are crippled by their awareness of others; they are paralysed by what everyone else thinks. But such people do no harm, on the whole . . . .

LW: But not much good either.

IM: Well, they could be saints. It is the people who have no sense, or little sense, that other people exist who do the harm.

LW: It's interesting that you've mentioned faces. One of the background texts that I'll be using in my book are the writings of the philosopher Emmanuel Lévinas. One of his central images is the face; he uses the face as a figure for ethical encounter between people, and he differentiates between the face and the mask, with social life being mainly composed of masks. When you recognize the other face to face, and this is a key image, you recognize that the other is just as vulnerable and defenseless in the world as you are, then you are no longer capable of committing violence against the other person. I've been reading Lévinas alongside your work and they work very well together. So, one of the things I'll be focusing on are actually face-to-face encounters; I'll take Lévinas's philosophical idea and literalize it, to a certain extent. I'm very interested in certain encounters in your work, particularly most recently between Henry Perowne and Baxter, when they're literally right in each other's faces, or to go back quite a way, I'm quite taken with the story 'Two Fragments', in one of your early collections, where you have that strange encounter between another Henry and that Chinese man at the end, lugging his dresser along, trying to get it up the stairs. There are a lot of encounters like that in your work, and it seems to me as a reader that these encounters are often quite staged. I'm also thinking of the cliff scene in *Amsterdam*, where you have Clive looking at the woman about to be raped. I wonder if you could talk about these scenes of moral encounter, where you have almost like a laboratory experiment, with two characters thrust together, almost nose-to-nose in some cases, trying to figure out how to deal with each other.

IM: I don't know Lévinas's work. Perhaps he belongs in the tradition of non-evidential literary theorizing. There are locations within the brain that are intimately connected with face recognition; we know this from patients who have suffered lesions in a particular area, who can't recognize the faces of people closest to them. It surely must be one of the fundamentals of any human encounter, to discover the intentions of the other; reading a face is about reading the immediate future. For that reason, I'm not sure I would make the distinction between the mask and the face. We are social creatures. There's nothing mask-like about our social presentation to the world, because social is what we are. We wither without the company of others. I'm not for a moment saying that Lévinas might not offer you a useful template for your purposes, but from my point of view, I would doubt the distinction between an essential and a social face.

So the social encounter seems to me a way into the heart of things, of people. As for the set pieces you mention, I hope that a sense of threat narrows the reader's attention and keeps expectations poised. I like the ways in which things can go out of control between people, I like a sense of open-ended peril, or edginess. It allows some play with the pulse of sentences, the drum-beat, with some kind of thickening, something of the heart quickening in the rhythm of the prose. But above all it's a mode of exploration. I'm not sure we can investigate ourselves in isolation. It's in the encounter, the encounter under pressure, the crisis between people, which reveals us to ourselves.

LW: Since you're talking about threat and encounters, I'd like to ask you specifically about the encounter between Henry Perowne and Baxter. When I first read the novel, I must admit that that encounter really troubled me; it perplexed me in some ways, in one specific way I'd like to ask you about. At a number of points in *Saturday*, you have Henry Perowne, or the narrator focalizing through Henry, identify people by culture or race very specifically: the three women in the burkhas, for instance, or the Cockney nurse, but Baxter is a blank, in a sense. I gave a paper on *Saturday* in July, when I was here in London, and some people came up at the end and said, "Baxter is black", of course he's black, and a number of other people came up and said, "No, he's white, he's a skinhead." It was interesting to hear how people had concretized the character so very differently. But that encounter with Baxter ends up with his being quite neutralized, in effect, with the threat kind of put away, and then the Perowne family can go on very happily, it seems.

IM: Do you mean at the very end?

LW: Yes, at the very end.

IM: But there's also the encounter in the street.

LW: I guess I mean both. But in both cases, you have the doctor really as the dominant force, able to use his scientific knowledge, his class, etc., as a kind of power over this character, and in the end Baxter is just crumpled, is operated on, and obviously just goes off to die a horrible death somewhere. He seems to do that off-stage in a way that, when I first read the novel, I must admit kind of troubled me. I wondered if you could talk about the relationship between those two characters, and how you felt that relationship playing out.

IM: Well, I never thought of him as black, and as for his social background, he was a lower middle-class boy from

Folkstone, who left school at 16, clever but frustrated, and deeply ill. The question is, how does a man who has all life's privileges and values his rationality, what does such a person do in the face of Baxter's aggression and irrationality? One thing a rational man does is try to save his own skin, and then start to fret about it—because he's trying to live a moral life. Perowne does think he's abused his authority. But what was the alternative? Take a beating from three men stronger than him, on the street? But every act has its consequences. Perowne ends up humiliating a man, and as his teenage son warns him, everyone has his pride. So he then faces a larger and much more dire situation when Baxter returns.

There's a literary convention by which it's incumbent on the novelist to redeem a character like Baxter — he's not really ill, or someone will save him or he'll see the error of his ways. But someone with severe Huntingdon's Disease is doomed. It is the modern equivalent in Greek tragedy of the curse of the oracle. All that is offered to Baxter is to be stirred by something Perowne himself is not, the rendering of "Dover Beach." Because he's highly volatile, for that's the nature of his disorder, his mood swings radically.

I wasn't writing an allegory or a parable—but there was always some sort of parallel in my mind between his situation and the larger situation which came to a head in London on July 7 this summer: the visitation of an extreme religious death-cult. How do we deal with it? Well, we might want to crush it. Or we might like to tell ourselves that the people who come bearing this are unfortunate, socially deprived, victims of this or that. Then we discover that the four July bombers were not poverty stricken or deprived, but quite well educated—and infected with a mad idea. We know that Islamic terrorists are not going to destroy Western civilization—even if they mounted a bomb attack every week. And yet, collectively, we feel we could be driven mad, into irrational acts of our own. In other words, those who have all the power, all the knowledge, all the access to the greatest violence, all the science and the technology, get flummoxed. We don't know what to do in the face of this kind of threat. To make ourselves more secure, we begin to think of limiting our own freedoms. As Perowne discovers, irrationality is infectious. In the Second World War, the Allies, in order to defeat Nazism, believed they had to become genocidal.

LW: He is reborn, though, to certain extent. I can't remember the exact wording, but there's an image when he's coming out of surgery where Perowne is cradling his head, almost as if he's a baby. I didn't know if that's meant to be ironic.

IM: No. It's never in doubt that by saving his life, he's consigning him to the path he must descend by. To go back to your sense of Baxter's emptiness: there is a simple rhetorical element that shouldn't be overlooked. This is a novel written from inside one character. I could only give the reader Baxter as he appears in the present to Perowne. All the other characters have a shared past with Henry which he can reflect on. I didn't spell it out, but in social terms, Baxter is clear enough . . .

LW: I guess I was thinking of that very strong parallel between Islamic terrorism, which is a cultural threat both domestically and internationally, as we discovered in July, that the threat is as much within England as without, and Baxter obviously is aligned with that kind of threat, which has certain cultural valences to it—of the Other, an uncontainable Other, a frightening Other, and he is described as being "simian." It is striking in the novel that there are so many other characters, even peripheral characters, people who are there just for a moment, are often described in very specific cultural terms. When Perowne looks at Baxter, none of that comes through.

IM: Well, when Perowne is looking at Baxter, that's all he sees; he doesn't see anything except culture, and feels a kind of visceral distaste. I'm trying to think what other characters there are that were . . . there aren't many characters in this book. The immediate family often are described in one way or another.

LW: There's Giulio.

IM: But he's off-stage.

LW: There's Andrea.

IM: The black girl. But I mean . . . I'm trying to get at your sense of emptiness in Baxter . . .

LW: Maybe emptiness wasn't the right way of phrasing it—a vagueness, perhaps, that I didn't feel with other characters in the novel.

IM: You know, there's a distant kind of literary ancestor for Baxter—it's Forster's Leonard Bast. There is a similar hunger in him. In the exchange he and Perowne have about available treatment for Huntingdon's, it's clear that Baxter has read the literature; he's not stupid. And he's actually very lonely with this, and the kind of company he keeps can offer no kind of solace.

LW: All right, well, why don't I leave poor Baxter alone for a moment? I'd like to go back to the binary between rationality and irrationality. I've read your introduction to that book that's coming out with all the famous scientists talking about what they believe to be true but can't prove. It brought together a number of ideas that I've been thinking about in your work, in terms of your endorsements in a number of your interviews of rationality, that reason is a good thing. I find that in your novels that reason is always very closely connected with irrationality; the example I was thinking of is when Perowne thinks of himself as a "witchdoctor delivering a curse" when he's diagnosing Baxter. Even at that moment of being most scientific, there's an irrational side to him. You use the phrase "magical thinking" quite frequently in your novels. I think I first noticed it in *The Child in Time*, which I read quite early on, a number of years ago, and I always pick up on it when I come across it again. I wondered if you could talk about how you see rationality and irrationality connected in your work, and whether or not you think of those forces at all in gendered terms. Sometimes, they seem to get played out that way—for instance, in *Black Dogs*.

IM: Yes, but sometimes it's reversed—Thelma in *The Child in Time* is a scientist. I don't think rationality is easy for us, as a species. Clearly, we're full of many other impulses: we're hierarchical and superstitious, we love ritual, our calculations of risk are often at odds with the figures, we understand each other with an emotional insight that is beyond the reach of logic. And language is full of magical connections. And yet, haltingly, over an immense stretch of time, let's say two and a half millennia, we have developed a thought-system, whose powers of explanation and prediction are clearly immense. Only science is able to correct its course constantly as its knowledge base grows and more evidence is gathered. Unlike religion, it thrives on scepticism and informed but hostile scrutiny. Its greatest achievements rank with the finest endeavours in the arts. It has delivered us from smallpox and the terror of believing that thunder is the wrath of the gods. But the technologies that have sprung from this cleverness have brought us nuclear weapons, climate change, and a mass culture that can seem loud and moronic. We've made this thing and yet it sits with us so uncomfortably. It goes against our grain—we still have these supernatural longings.

You often hear people say that science and religion describe two entirely different realms, that there is no conflict between them. I disagree. Religions describe the world. Was Mohammed instructed by God to write the Koran? Was Jesus the son of God? Was the world invented by dreaming snakes? Or subterranean spirits? Is there a benign spirit who listens to your special pleas and acts on them to affect the future to deliver your child from illness or get you through your exams? These are questions about the world.

Consciously or not, I find I've played around with these questions, either within or between my characters. It fascinates me. Perhaps if you left the planet in a spaceship for a good while you might find these tensions endearing in the species—we need and love the fruits of our rationality, but it appalls us too, or make us suspicious. I don't think we will ever talk ourselves into letting go of the sky-gods. Nor will our social organization ever satisfy the rational dreamer—we are simply not written that way.

LW: I haven't asked you about *Atonement*. You've talked in other interviews about your efforts to maintain a balance between literary texts that are conscious of themselves as texts, and some kind of realistic inner world. With *Atonement* in particular, because there are so many layers within layers, it became more complex for me as a reader to keep my finger on what was 'really' happening, in those terms. I was struck Briony's doodle in her notebook, "There was an old lady who swallowed a fly," from the nursery rhyme. It seemed to me that that was how the novel itself was constructed, like a recursive rhyme almost, with layer upon layer, and I wonder if you could talk for a moment about you felt that sort of intense self-consciousness plays itself out in that novel, I think more so than in any of the other books, what kind of effect that has on your desire to create a sort of persuasive realism. I don't mean that term in a strictly nineteenth-century sense, but with reference to some sort of convincing textual world.

IM: The recursive, or self-referential or intertextual in literature has to be embedded in the warmth of the real, the warmly living. Otherwise, it's dull and dry. In fact, all these elements that postmodern critics like to discuss only arise with any interest if they grow out of the effort, the sweat of passionate commitment to creating the humanly real—that's when the business of making the artifice spills into the very thing it describes. I've said before that I believe that the best sentence is always aware of itself, almost as if it contains the instructions or the blueprint for its own construction. The best sentences in Updike, or Bellow, or Nabokov have a playful air. Perhaps that's why the greatest lines seem to have a hint of comedy about them. But such sentences are still true, accurate, and we feel a thrill of recognition because we all share a world that exists beyond the subjective, and we love to read it truthfully rendered. In *Atonement*, the moment I decided to include a young girl in love with writing, everything else, the intertextuality, the lifetime of successive drafts, just followed, rather in the service of realism.

LW: Let me ask you about optimism. I'm quite intrigued by the number of comic endings your novels have. I mean that in a fairly traditional sense.

IM: Comic?

LW: Yes, comic. I'm thinking of *The Child in Time*, which ends with the birth of a baby, or *Saturday*, which has, I think, essentially a comic ending. We talked about Baxter—he doesn't end very comically—but the main characters do. I was struck in *Saturday* by the strong sense of optimism that Henry Perowne expresses, particularly through the scientists that he quotes, Darwin and Peter Medawar, "To deride the hopes of progress is the ultimate fatuity." I wonder if you have a sense of yourself as a comic writer, or as an optimistic writer, or perhaps even at times as a utopian writer.

IM: I'll take the last one first. I'm not a utopian writer. Once they start to act politically, utopianists are people to be feared, with all their talk of breaking eggs to make omelettes. One strand of *Saturday* was the expression of a degree of impatience with the professionalisation of despair, very common among liberal arts intellectuals. In private they will confess to an enormous range of appetites and pleasures in life, but none of this seems to have a place in their bleak worldview. Pessimism is intellectually delicious, an intellectual's badge of seriousness. We have to be able to encompass both the terrible aspects that the world presents—climate change and poverty above all—and that fact that historically, we in the West are having the time of our lives, as it were. In unprecedented numbers, we have access to extraordinary machines, material well-being as well as intellectual freedoms that did not exist until the waning of Christianity. But my writing has been dark enough, I've been criticized for that. As you get older, you perhaps lose the reckless, destructive streak that once felt exhilarating. You want the human project to succeed. Perhaps this is what draws me to science—satisfying curiosity is at heart an optimistic pursuit. I'm with Medawar—total pessimism is one more luxury of the over-fattened West.

I'm not quite sure what you mean when you say that *Saturday* has a comic ending, or *The Child in Time*. In that novel, a child is lost and a child is born; one cannot replace the other. *Atonement* has a sombre ending—a woman facing oblivion, facing the fact that she has falsified the truth in her final draft, possibly out of fear, possibly because she loves fiction too much. And *Saturday* is ambiguous in this respect—a man climbs into bed beside his sleeping wife after brooding at the window, contemplating his own declining powers, his children leaving home, his mother about to die, and how he might leave the city with all the faint hearts to escape terrorism; as he falls asleep all that really remains for him—and it's a big "all"—is love for his wife. It's hard to bow out of a novel.

LW: I've always suspected that.

IM: There's the little, ambiguous, minor gesture that can seem so fey. There's the thunderous gathering-up of strands. Between preciousness and pomposity there's only a narrow space. Writers are often deeply moved to reach the end of their books, and that's when they overreach. Readers aren't necessarily moved to reach the end of a book. Writers need to do at least one final stony-hearted revision, unmoved by the trumpets and massed strings.

LW: I want to ask you what you think the role of writers is these days as public intellectuals. You wrote something for *The Guardian* right away after the July bombings, you spoke out publicly after the 9/11 attacks in the United States. Do you see yourself doing more of that kind of thing? Is that something that you feel it's important for writers to do?

IM: I have mixed feelings about it. What I wrote after 9/11 and July 7th were a novelist's take—no analysis, no reflections on Islam or terror or international politics, so much as what I imagined it was like in the planes, or on the street. We have noisy, opinion-rich media. Novelists, in one of the minor leagues of celebrity culture, can get drawn in to lend their voices to the babble. Sometimes I can't resist—it's too interesting—but mostly I say no. That quiet, driven state of mind you need to be in to write a novel rather works against being in public spaces. Seneca wrote that "he who is known to many people is not known to himself."

LW: I've taught a number of courses on Rushdie, and the last course I taught I actually focused on him as a public intellectual. We did some fiction as well, but we did all his essays and his interventions with the press. It was an interesting discussion, because we don't tend to think of writers as public intellectuals anymore. You're telling me that the demand for that is actually quite high.

IM: The machine is always hungry. Every request comes by e-mail now, right on to the desk where you're trying to do your own work. But we live in interesting times. Religion, war, terrorism, climate change, and always literature, science, music. There's so much to engage with in the public arena, and so much to learn. But how to preserve private space in the context of all the chatter is difficult.

11

OTHER WRITINGS

In the Preface to *A Move Abroad*, McEwan conveys the surprise he felt in 1987 when reviewers responded to the publication of *The Child in Time* by saying that he was "breaking a six year silence" in writing since *The Comfort of Strangers*: "From my point of view there was no silence, only a tactical evasion, a move abroad; the novel is a capacious form, but not everything is appropriate to it" (xxvi). During that hiatus, McEwan had continued to write, particularly screenplays for television and the cinema. In 1981, he published together three television plays—*Jack Flea's Birthday Celebration* (1976), *Solid Geometry* (1978, based on the story of the same name, originally written in 1973, from *First Love, Last Rites*), and *The Imitation Game* (1978)—as *The Imitation Game and Other Plays. The Imitation Game*, which McEwan characterizes as "a polemic about gender and power" (MA xxiv), is set in England during the Second World War in the intelligence community, a secretive world that exposes the systematic exclusion of women from full participation in society outside the domestic sphere. McEwan felt that the dramatic form made possible a "more mimetic, a more narrowly accurate representation of the surface of social existence than that afforded by the novel with all its conventional freedoms of, for example, authorial intrusion and the highly artificial depiction of the inner life" (MA xxiv). The focus on outward social interaction made possible by on-screen dialogue also suited McEwan's purposes in writing *The Ploughman's Lunch*, released as a feature film in 1983, in which he dramatizes the "new spirit" of Britain under

Margaret Thatcher's government: "Money-obsessed, aggressively competitive and individualistic, contemptuous of the weak, vindictive towards the poor . . . indifferent to the environment, deeply philistine, enamoured of policemen, soldiers and weapons" (*MA* xxiv). To convey another disturbing aspect of the political reality of the early 1980s, the threat of nuclear annihilation, McEwan adopted a different form, the oratorio, a non-dramatic choral work traditionally based on a religious theme, but in the case of *Or Shall We Die?* (1982), having a "secular" and "moral" (*MA* 7) orientation. McEwan published *The Ploughman's Lunch* and the oratorio together as *A Move Abroad* in 1983, claiming that both pieces lay the "groundwork" (*MA* vii) for the critique of moral and environmental degradation in *The Child in Time*. In both *The Imitation Game and Other Plays* and *A Move Abroad*, McEwan fit the form of his writing more closely to the subject matter, ranging from gender conflict to global issues, deliberately stepping away from the novel during a period of intense social and political change.

As Jack Slay Jr notes, McEwan's first screenplays "were closely aligned in both theme and content to his early stories" (89). In his introduction to *The Imitation Game and Other Plays*, McEwan explains that he saw in the screenplay a way of capturing the "scale" and "intimacy" of short fiction, with its "highly selective detail" and "rapid establishment of people and situations" (9), in another form. With *Jack Flea's Birthday Celebration* and *Solid Geometry*, he also set out "to kick over the traces" of the "naturalistic" (*IG* 10) conventions of television by carrying over the bizarre subject matter and experimental techniques of his early work. Like many of the short stories and *The Cement Garden*, these two screenplays focus on unusual situations and characters in enclosed domestic settings that expose the repressed underside of normal domestic life.

Jack Flea's Birthday Celebration, first aired in 1976, was written just after McEwan had completed *First Love, Last Rites*, and he has said that he sees the play as "really belonging in that volume" (*IG* 10), which suggests an thematic affinity that goes beyond generic differences. The main character David is dominated by women, in this case not only by his mother but also by his intimate partner, Ruth. She and David play a trick on his parents when they come to celebrate his birthday and to meet her for the first time. First,

David reads to them from the ersatz manuscript (really just blank paper) of a novel that he is supposedly writing about a boy, Jack Flea, who runs away from home to escape his "miserably ineffec- tual father" and "stifling, sinister" mother, and who takes up with a "fantasy mother" (*IG* 38) who pampers him. This latter role is then taken up by Ruth, who spends the evening feeding David with a spoon, pretending to usurp the maternal privilege of the over- bearing Mrs Lee, with David playing along as an infantilized adult, regressing to babyhood like Tom in *The Cement Garden*. Although the ruse against the parents is revealed before they leave, the final shot turns the tables by showing David being tucked up in an over- sized cot in a separate bedroom by Ruth. Her prompt to him "Let's go to bed" (48) once they are alone is not a sexual invitation but a parental imperative—she even "*shushes*" (49, italics in original) him when he tries to speak.

This ending suggests that David, like so many of McEwan's early characters, is complicit in his subjugation: the stage direc- tions state that Ruth and David "*kiss deeply*" (49, italics in original) when she tucks him in, and he stays put and is quiet. His dimin- ished masculine identity, reflected in his browbeaten father and choice of "Flea" for his protagonist's last name, is also symbol- ized, in Slay's view, by the "blank page" (94) of his non-existent novel. David's effort to assert his autonomy and express himself creatively by making up his story serves, McEwan notes in his introduction, as a "self-reflecting fiction" that turns "fantasy" into "reality," the sort of experimental strategy that "writers new to a form are tempted to exploit" (11). The audience is lured into the deception of this mise-en-abyme by watching David at the begin- ning type the title of the play they are about to watch, text that later vanishes off the page, just as David's story about male sub- mission to female domination gets absorbed into the real scenario of his life.

The original story 'Solid Geometry' centers on a misogynistic protagonist who treats women as disposable objects; in this case, an unnamed male narrator (called Albert in the screenplay) makes his wife Maisie literally disappear. Albert and Maisie exemplify the conventionally gendered rationalist/mystic split familiar from other McEwan texts such as *Black Dogs*, with the man fascinated by science and mathematics and especially his great-grandfather's diaries, and the woman trying to get her "head straight" (*IG* 72) by hanging about the house, interpreting her dreams and reading Tarot cards. Ryan notes that, "in the interval between writing the tale in 1973 and reworking it for television five years later, McEwan's ideas about gender and power had become much more sharply defined" (1994: 27), a shift evident in the later version. In the story we hear only the perspective of the cerebral, rationalistic first-person male narrator, relieved only by excerpts from his great-grandfather's multi-volume diary, whereas in the screenplay Maisie has the opportunity to speak for herself, making her a far more sympathetic character, McEwan believes (*IG* 13). This more dialogic format, with its "strong narrative line" showing the interrelationships between Maisie and Albert, and Albert's great-grandfather and his friend Maxwell ("M" in the original) made *Solid Geometry*, according to McEwan "a far better play than a short story" (*IG* 13–14).

Solid Geometry, which the BBC decided to keep off the air in 1979 on the grounds that it had "grotesque and bizarre sexual elements" (*IG* 14), was eventually produced in 2003 by Scottish television, with a new screenplay by Denis Lawson, who also directed. The screenplay begins with Albert's great-grandfather attending a country auction in 1875 with Maxwell. This event is merely reported in the story, but the television version gives it historical immediacy; the auctioneer's comment that the sale can proceed only once "all the ladies" (*IG* 53) have left the room establishes a context of female exclusion. In both the story and play, the great-grandfather bids successfully, on the advice of his friend, for the preserved penis of one Captain Nicholls who died in prison some years before (1873 in the story, 1835 in the play, making it more of a relic). In both cases this phallic object serves as a symbol of masculine power, as well as of the sexual fulfillment that Maisie is denied, leading her to destroy the glass jar in a rage; yet the way in which she responds to her husband's disposal of the penis is different in each text. The story reports her as giggling and asking "What happened to it anyway? Did you suck it off?" (*FLLR* 49) versus her line in the play: "What happened to it anyway? Did you eat it?" (*IG* 87). The former, conveyed by the narrator, suggests an assumed erotic playfulness on her part, while the latter, spoken by herself, conveys through double entendre both fellatio and cannibalism, the implication being that Maisie is worried that Albert is trying to internalize the power of the phallic symbol.

The second item that the great-grandfather nearly purchases at the auction raises similar distinctions between the texts. In the story, the item for bid is "the unnamed portion of the late Lady Barrymore," and the narrator reports simply that M "dissuaded" (*FLLR* 31) his friend from the purchase. The screenplay, on other hand, devotes considerable attention to this object, which is described as difficult to identify in its "murky" (*IG* 55) jar of liquid. The great-grandfather longs to own this "priceless item with aristocratic connections," as the auctioneer touts it, and to put "the female counterpart to Captain Nicholls" (*IG* 55) on his mantelpiece next to the other specimen. Maxwell physically restrains his friend from bidding, claiming "It's badly preserved, *whatever it is*, and therefore quite worthless" (56, my italics), while the auctioneer congratulates another bidder, Sam Israel, on his "handsome acquisition" (56).

The anxiety surrounding this vaginal symbol emanates in two directions in the screenplay. In the nineteenth-century narrative line, there is a strong suggestion of homoerotic desire between the great-grandfather and Maxwell, who discuss the scholarly opinion of various sexual positions, including "*a posteriori*" (61, italics in original) entry and the multiple positions detailed by "Romano, a pupil of the distinguished Raphael" and "Mr Forberg" (67), the latter being Friedrich Karl Forberg (1770–1848), whose essay *De Figuris Veneris* inspired paintings of homosexual lovemaking and bestiality, as well as of sex between men and women. Although this discussion is reported in a neutral way in the story, in the play it forms part of the intimate conversation in the great-grandfather's study during which he and Maxwell get drunk on wine and end up, according to the stage directions, "*laughing helplessly*," with the great-grandfather "*helping MAXWELL undress*" (88, italics in original). In the present timeline, Maisie's vagina becomes a site of avoidance and repression; the story's narrator wonders if she destroys the preserved phallus because "she wanted to make love" or "she wanted a penis" (*FLLR* 49), suggesting the traditional Freudian notion of penis envy, whereas the screenplay does not include that speculation. Rather, the focus of the play's action is on Maisie's efforts to save her marriage by making gentle apologies, performing conventional feminine tasks such as cooking, and attempting to communicate with Albert on romantic and personal terms. As in the story, she tries to share her recurrent nightmares about "thousands of babies heaped up" (*IG* 58), only to be ignored repeatedly by her husband; this dream expresses a deeply felt pain on her part for the lack of a child, a reality made more vivid by her announcement in both texts that her period has just started, indicating that she is not pregnant. In both the story and the screenplay, we learn of M's/Maxwell's correspondence with the father of an American mathematician named Goodman who had developed a "cyclical theory of menstruation" (*FLLR* 40, *IG* 75), evidence of a masculine attempt to rationalize and control the natural activities of the female body.

The two timelines, with their parallel couple relationships, combine to produce a scenario of profound anxiety about female sexuality. Movement between the two is made possible on the screen by the device of the glowing diary, which also gives access to the third time-frame, the conference of the mathematicians in Vienna a year before the discussions of the great-grandfather and Maxwell. From this conference, Maxwell learns of the fantastical demonstration of a geometrical discovery, "the plane without a surface" (*IG* 78), which when adapted to the human form causes the person to disappear, as he verifies by experimenting on Maxwell. Slay notes that Albert must take on some of Maisie's characteristics, making use of the "antirational" (95) to rid himself of her. In the screenplay, McEwan stresses that Maisie's desire, both for sex and for romantic companionship, is what leads to her demise; she speaks at some length about her experience of finding "a little secret place" (*IG* 92) by the river that she wants to share with Albert, while his duplicitous efforts to contort her body are to be made to "*look as much as possible like a scene of lovemaking*" (91, italics in original), according to the stage directions. While the story ends with the narrator reporting his "trance"-like state as he coolly admires the aesthetic quality of the "positioning of her limbs" (*FLLR* 51), the television version leaves us with the voices of the frightened Maisie asking as she vanishes "Al, where am I?" and the great-grandfather frantically calling "Where are you Maxwell?" (*IG* 93). The dramatic structure of the screenplay, with its double timeline and clear contrast between the couples, emphasizes McEwan's indictment of anti-female hatred.

After the shock endings and "dazzling electronic techniques" (*IG* 13) of his first two screenplays, McEwan was ready to write a more conventional television screenplay. He describes *The*

Imitation Game as "not formally experimental at all," noting that he "had begun to think there might be more effective, if well tried, means of trying to regard the world afresh" (*IG* 10). Once he had finished *The Cement Garden* in August 1977, he found himself increasingly interested in the implications of the Women's Movement, but felt "dissatisfaction" (*IG* 16) with fiction as a means of conveying those ideas. Although he believed that some of his short stories and *The Cement Garden* expressed to some extent the ways in which "patriarchy corrupts our most intimate relationships with comic and tragic consequences," he also found that in his work to date he had used narrators who were "too idiosyncratic or solipsistic" (*IG* 16) to allow him to present the range of societal points of view that he wanted to explore. The dramatic form of *The Imitation Game* made it possible for him to reframe the debate about gender roles as a dialogue among men and women confronting the massive changes in the domestic workforce necessitated by the war, with the patriarchal values of that time providing context and contrast for the contemporary situation.

In the central character Cathy Raine, McEwan creates a prototypical, though somewhat anachronistic, feminist heroine trying to break through the barriers of a male-dominated world in 1940 by joining the Auxiliary Territorial Service (ATS) as part of the Ultra project, assigned to decipher German secret codes. By choosing to do intelligence work, she avoids being "directed" (*IG* 99) into a nearby munitions factory by her authoritarian father, having to marry her priggish fiancé Tony, and enduring the tedium of her small town, where nothing ever happens. The recurrent image of the mirror, in which Cathy checks her reflection, provides a visual marker of her efforts to transform her identity, while the presence throughout the screenplay of pianos, sometimes locked up and inaccessible, on which she tries to perfect Mozart's difficult Fantasia K475 creates an auditory correlative of her challenge to improve herself. Cathy longs to be "*doing* something" (*IG* 110) active, and thinks of the war and even a potential German occupation as opportunities to develop her skills and independence in ways that would not otherwise be available to her. In his introduction, McEwan notes not only the sense of "great camaraderie" (*IG* 19) that many women enjoyed during the war, but also the persistent efforts of the military establishment to characterize them as untrustworthy, emotionally and physically weak, and incapable of intellectual work. This societal perspective is articulated in the screenplay in the form of a voice-over spoken by a senior ATS officer, along with the sound of wireless reports exhorting women to contribute to the war effort by extending their domestic chores of cooking and cleaning to the support of the troops. The wireless reporter speaks verbatim the slogan that McEwan discovered in a document in the Imperial War Museum library: "No skilled person is to do what can be done by an unskilled person, and no man is to do what can be done by a woman" (*IG* 19, 151). Cathy rebels against these limitations, trying to crack the enemy codes on her own time, and finally being reassigned to domestic duties at Bletchley Park, "the centre of it all" (*IG* 137), after assaulting a publican who tries to force her and her friend Mary out of his establishment for posing a sexual distraction to the men.

McEwan explains that he came to understand the Ultra project, with its "concentric rings" of secrecy, as "a microcosm, not only of the war but of a whole society" (*IG* 20). While the societal model invoked in the play is specifically based on gender, McEwan believes that it can also represent other kinds of repressive structures; in his interview with John Haffenden, he describes *The Imitation Game* as "an allegory ... about the way systems exclude individuals" (174). As Cathy moves further into this system, she breaches more of the boundaries designed to keep women marginalized, and in the process becomes increasingly endangered. Tony's characterization of the ATS women as being like "ants" (120) reflects somewhat ironically on this hive-like structure, since the "queen" at the centre takes the form of the women who provide the pretext for military violence in defence of a traditional notion of domestic life, which in turn is detrimental to them. Women such as Cathy who have defied their conventional roles are also associated in the play with "pigs" (127), their dirtiness a product of their sexual liberty, as evidenced by the women's bullying one of their roommates in the ATS dormitory, Sarah, who is called a "stinker" (134) for her promiscuity. Like Maisie in *Solid Geometry* Cathy, too, is punished for her sexuality; when John Turner, an intelligence officer, tells her she "can't refuse" his proposition, she replies to herself "No" (164), implying either that she feels coerced or that her desire to sleep with him is strong. The latter scenario seems more likely once we witness Turner's tirade after his failure to perform, in which he accuses her of being sexually experienced, suggesting that she has been highly responsive in bed. With this reversal, Cathy discovers the deepest secret of all—that behind the façade of masculine supremacy, whether military or erotic, men are fallible human beings. The link between masculinity and the vulnerability of the state is reinforced by Cathy's conviction as a spy and imprisonment, her ultimate expulsion from a society that feels threatened by her desire to penetrate and reform structures of power.

Along with the circles of secrecy, the centralizing image in the screenplay is the "imitation game" devised by Alan Turing, a mathematician who served at Bletchley Park and who later played a key role in the development of computers. The "game," as McEwan describes it in his introduction and Turner repeats it in the play, is designed to determine the intellectual capacity of a machine. To begin, a man and a woman are put in separate rooms, and communicate with an interrogator (male or female) through a teleprinter. The interrogator's aim is "to find out which of the two is a man, and which is the woman. The object of the man is to try and cause the interrogator to make a wrong identification, while the woman's purpose is to help the interrogator" (153). In both cases, then, the participants are trying to convince the interrogator that they are the woman, which should lead both parties to express conventionally feminine ideas. Turing's original question, "Can Machines Think?" (17), would enter into the scenario if the man were to be replaced with a mechanical respondent, which would be challenged to characterize itself as female. McEwan uses this illustration of Turing's problem to create the opportunity for one of his characters, an officer named Matthews, to make a sexist joke: "Shouldn't you first establish whether the woman can think?" (154). Beyond that, though, the metaphor of the imitation game illuminates the gender dynamics of the social world represented in the television play. Cathy is punished for inadequately expressing conventional feminine characteristics, and for "imitating" men through her drive for deeper knowledge and a more active, engaging life. The men, on the other hand, spend their time constructing a masculine game, with secret colours—"Red's up!" (155), shouts a young mathematician—and codes accessible only to them. Turner thinks of Cathy, frustrated with being confined to domestic chores, as an "intriguing" (163) mystery to be deciphered. Gender itself is presented in the screenplay as a series of intricate codes to be broken and analysed by the characters and audience alike, one aspect of a societal game with serious consequences for both men and women retrospectively clear in the patriarchal and militaristic world of the 1940s, but still evident in the late 1970s even after feminism's effects were beginning to be felt.

In *The Ploughman's Lunch*, McEwan wanted to focus more directly on contemporary issues, setting out to capture the "textures of everyday London" (*MA* 26) in the early 1980s, especially the ruthless competitiveness inspired by Prime Minister Thatcher's free-market policies. The spirit of the times is personified by the main character, James Penfield, a self-absorbed journalist who will stop at nothing to achieve his personal and professional aims. He ignores his own dying mother, yet has no scruples about sleeping with Ann Barrington, whose daughter Susan he has been pursuing sexually, in order to secure information for the book he is writing on the history of the Suez Crisis in 1956. McEwan had had an interest in the Crisis since his childhood, when he and his family were stationed in Libya and he had watched his father participate in the protection of British military families: "I understood for the first time that political events were real and affected people's lives—they were not just stories in the papers that grown-ups read" (*MA* 27). In later years, McEwan came to understand that the Crisis, with its diminishment of Britain as a world power, had been more than a political defeat; it had become "an affair of the heart, of who we thought we were, who we wanted to be" (*MA* 29). By 1981, McEwan saw the Crisis as revelatory of the nationalistic narrative being crafted with "steely pragmatism" (*MA* 28) by the Thatcher government to serve its own ends. The story of reconstructed British supremacy was given more currency by the Falklands invasion in 1982, which serves as a subtle backdrop to the film's action, but is also reinforced through visual clues, such as when James walks by a bank of "Space Invader" (60) video game machines.

Through his role as amateur historian in the film, James embodies the work of historical revisionism by the state under Thatcherism that McEwan exposes in *The Ploughman's Lunch*. McEwan constructed the screenplay such that all of the major characters are people "involved professionally in shaping our concepts of ourselves as citizens and as a nation" (*MA* 28); James's approach as a journalist to the writing of history is deliberately put in conflict with that of the socialist historian Ann, who, following the ideas of Czech writer Milan Kundera, believes that every member of society must participate in the "struggle of memory against forgetting" (76). James starts out wanting to write a book about the Crisis that would "set out the events as they happened" (45), but the dismissive attitude of the editor Gold, who pays more attention to his expensive lunch and shopping, reveals the capitalist priorities of Thatcherite Britain. In the end, Gold is satisfied with the financially successful but superficial book that James has written, which he proclaims "a very good read" (118). The decline in James's values as a researcher is associated with the general degradation of journalism as a profession. Ann recalls how her first husband, who worked for the BBC, fought to preserve journalistic independence during the Crisis; in the 1980s, stories about world politics and human rights are suppressed in favour of pieces on "tits, bingo, jingo, horoscope, sport, celebs, gossip" (68), as James's fellow journalist Jeremy puts it, anticipating the editorial principles of Vernon Halliday in *Amsterdam*.

The descent of journalism into tabloid sensationalism coincides with the rise of commercialism as a formative influence on cultural and historical consciousness, a force incarnated in the screenplay by Ann's second husband Matthew, a director of commercials. A master manipulator of the past, he cites his advertising campaign for a "new lager" as the reason the lineage of British monarchs remains "alive and well in the national memory" (92), and he explains to James the provenance of the ploughman's lunch, invented by advertisers to convince people to eat in pubs, "a completely successful fabrication of the past" (107). For McEwan, this bit of trivia provided the perfect "controlling metaphor" for this text, pointing to the "uses we make of the past, and the dangers, to an individual as well as a nation, of living without a sense of history" (26). The insidious effects of the erosion of historical awareness are vividly exemplified in the commercial that Matthew is making use of actors to simulate a *"deeply contented pre-war middle-class"* (105) family in its sitting room, with the mother happily serving hot drinks to her husband and children; this image conceals behind nostalgic sentimentality the gender inequality so evident in the wartime environment of *The Imitation Game* and still apparent in the present, as suggested by signs of Matthew's infidelity with a younger woman moments after the shoot has ended.

While *The Ploughman's Lunch* deals with social issues on a broader scale than *The Imitation Game*, it too draws connections between male dominance and political control. James and Matthew, with their callous indifference to the women in their lives, represent the elite of contemporary British society, with money and influence, whereas the female peace activists whose camp James stumbles upon in the woods are easily dismissed by the establishment as "vegetarians, hippies, disturbed housewives" (89). Susan, on the other hand, plays the role of the woman complicit with the oppressive system, choosing between "two paths," "power or not-power" (41), and strategically using her sexuality to get ahead as a journalist. Prime Minister Thatcher, the "Iron Lady," appears as a character in the film, articulating the imperialist ideology of British global superiority; her specific characterization, unlike her ungendered counterpart in *The Child in Time*, underscores power as a masculinist attribute, regardless of the sex of the leader.

The Prime Minister's propagandistic speech serves as the appropriate backdrop for James's realization that his friend Jeremy has started a relationship with Susan behind his back. McEwan notes in his introduction to the screenplay that he set out to create an analogy between the political and the personal, with James "unconsciously act[ing] out in his private life a sequence of betrayals and deceits" (*MA* 28) that parallel the political events of the Crisis, with the "unholy alliance between Britain, France and Israel over the Suez Affair . . . matched in the characters of the film" (Haffenden 187). The association between the Suez Crisis as an "affair of the heart" and the characters' romantic entanglement is underscored by the voice of the lecturer to whom James listens throughout the text, both in person and on tape, who contemplates the similarities between the moral responsibilities of individuals and of nations. The conclusion of this screenplay, as of *The Imitation Game*, is large collective structures in conflict with one another often mirror more intimate relationships between people, and that the dynamics of gender are visible on both the personal and political levels.

McEwan once again uses gender roles to represent larger societal issues in *Or Shall We Die?*, the oratorio about the nuclear threat set to music by Michael Berkley, with the central voices of an unnamed woman and man presenting two competing visions of the world: "No characters, no psychology, no actors pretending to be other people, simply voices articulating profoundest fears and some hope" (MA 6). In his introduction, McEwan associates the "female principle" with the creative imagination of Einsteinian physics, with its subjective sense of the interconnectedness and mutability of all things in the universe, and the "male principle" with the objective, rationalistic thinking of Newtonian physics (MA 15). While the female voice in the piece is attuned to spirituality, creativity and the environment, the male is the spokesperson for militarism, state power and violence. The woman's part is modeled after the words of a Japanese woman, Mrs Tomoyasu, whose young daughter was killed in 1945 by the American bombing of Hiroshima, an event celebrated by the male speaker and his related chorus: "Our God is manly! In war he refuses us nothing!" (19). Finally, the woman expresses the text's central question: "Shall there be womanly times, or shall we die?" (23).

McEwan returns to this sort of polarized gender dynamic in his most recent work, the libretto for Michael Berkley's opera *For You* (2008). The text centres on a domineering man, the egotistical composer Charles Frieth, who bears a resemblance to Amsterdam's Clive Linley, and the women he oppresses. The operatic language is particularly well suited to express the intense emotional conflict between the philandering creative genius, his long-suffering wife Antonia, and their Polish housekeeper Maria, who is hopelessly in love with her master and kills his wife to please him, a murder for which he is blamed.

McEwan's 'moves abroad' from the novel in these various texts primarily from the early to mid-1980s demonstrate his commitment to finding the appropriate forms in which to convey the power relationships, both personal and collective, that he has found to be worth exploring at certain historical moments. The experimentalism of *Jack Flea's Birthday Celebration* and *Solid Geometry* translated successfully into the television play, while the political subject matter of *The Imitation Game, The Ploughman's Lunch* and *Or Shall We Die?* was brought dramatically alive on the screen and the stage. After a long return to the novel, McEwan has once again departed from that form with the libretto *For You*. In all cases, these texts are proof of McEwan's ability to give us imaginative access to many points of view and their failure to be understood by one another.

12

CRITICAL RECEPTION

Since he began publishing, McEwan has been the focus of considerable attention from critics and reviewers alike, and their responses to his work have increased in proportion to his fame. The well-maintained website http://www.ianmcewan.com has an exhaustive listing of McEwan's primary texts, as well as of critical books, articles and reviews, including translations and secondary sources in languages other than English, many of which are hyperlinked. In this chapter, I present a selected list of sources that have been helpful to me in my work on McEwan and recommend some texts for further reading.

MONOGRAPHS

Dominic Head, *Ian McEwan*

Manchester and New York: Manchester University Press, 2007

This book covers McEwan's fiction up to and including *Saturday*, and touches on the major screenplays. Head begins by challenging the "problematic" claim that McEwan is "possibly the most significant of a number of writers ... who have resuscitated the link between morality and the novel for a whole generation" (1). The generation in question is that which witnessed the growing amorality caused by "the growth of self-interest, the expansion of corporate power and the collapse of the Welfare State"—in short, the period of the Thatcher administration and its aftermath—leading writers such as McEwan, Graham Swift, Martin Amis and Kazuo Ishiguro to attempt "to forge (or resuscitate) the moral impulse in a period that was not conducive to such a venture" (2). Head is convinced that McEwan's "extended fictional project" has an affinity with contemporary "narrative ethics," which he sees as "rescuscitat[ing] an older conviction about the moral content of fiction, but with the hindsight bestowed by poststructuralist thinking" (24). The role of characters in providing points of ethical identification is central to Head's argument, and he situates McEwan's views on character-creation within the contexts of postmodern theories of subjectivity and language, and evolutionary biology, which bear on McEwan's conception of how identity is formed. While Head is rightly wary about how McEwan's self-conscious "literary effects" (17) influence readers in the moral messages they take from his texts, he is more sanguine than I about the possibility of "consolation" (11), in the terms of Iris Murdoch's moral philosophy, resulting from McEwan's most recent fiction.

Peter Childs, *Ian McEwan's Enduring Love*

London and New York: Routledge, 2007

This book is indispensable to a study of one of McEwan's most challenging novels. Childs begins by providing important contexts for *Enduring Love,* including literary intertexts from the Romantic period and the seventeenth century, and key texts on evolutionary biology that influenced McEwan's creation of Joe: E.O. Wilson's *On Human Nature* (1978), Steven Pinker's *The Language Instinct* (1994), Robert Wright's *The Moral Animal* (1995) and so on. As is evident in my chapter on the novel, the critical readings by Kiernan Ryan, Sean Matthews, Childs himself and others are thought-provoking, and I highly recommend them. Finally, Childs gives an insightful interpretation of the 2004 film made of the novel, and leaves the reader with suggestions for further study.

Peter Childs, *The Fiction of Ian McEwan: A Reader's Guide to Essential Criticism*

London: Palgrave Macmillan, 2006

This compendium of critical excerpts, which covers the novels up to and including *Saturday* and includes insightful commentary from Childs, is a highly useful aid to the student or scholar of McEwan's work.

Claudia Schemberg, *Achieving "At-one-ment": Storytelling and the Concept of the Self in Ian McEwan's* The Child in Time, Black Dogs, Enduring Love *and* Atonement

Frankfurt: Peter Lang, 2004

Working from McEwan's own neologism "at-one-ment," Schemberg studies "the various ways the characters and narrators in the four novels structure their world, endow it with meaning, and strive for 'at-one-ment' in their lives" (9–10). They do so, she argues, through storytelling, which is a crucial element in the creation of moral selfhood. Like Head, she draws on ethical critics and philosophers such as Wayne C. Booth, Richard Rorty and Martha Nussbaum, to establish the parameters of discussing self-hood in a postmodern context. As Chapter 8 shows, I take issue with Schemberg's reading of *Atonement*, which accepts Briony's act of repentance as sincere without adequately taking into account the novel's complex narrative structure. Her response to this particular novel reflects a general tendency in her study to treat characters as endowed with a form of selfhood equivalent to that of flesh-and-blood people; as a result, she sometimes loses sight of their structural roles in the narratives in which they appear, and of the ironic edge that McEwan hones in so much of his work.

David Malcolm, *Understanding Ian McEwan*

Columbia, South Carolina: University of South Carolina Press, 2002

This critical study, which covers McEwan's work up to *Amsterdam*, is organized around what Malcolm sees as the five key issues in McEwan's work: textual self-consciousness, feminism, rationalism and science, moral perspective, and the "fragmentariness" of his novels. Malcolm provides a good introduction to McEwan's work, accessible to students at all levels. For more advanced readers, however, the structural rigidity of the five issues, carried throughout the chapters, becomes distracting and tends to reduce unnecessarily the complexity of McEwan's work. There is virtually no engagement here with the many concepts of literary theory from the past few decades so germane to the field of contemporary fiction.

Jack Slay, Jr. *Ian McEwan*

New York: Twayne, 1996

This early study provides a good thematic introduction to McEwan's work, up to and including *Black Dogs*, with a focus on male–female relationships, which Slay cites as the author's "principal concern" (6). It has particularly strong chapters on McEwan's short fiction and his screenplays. Slay makes good use of McEwan's early interviews and reviews, but his bibliography reveals the paucity of criticism available in the mid-1990s. This study also shies away from theoretical explorations of McEwan's work.

Kiernan Ryan. *Ian McEwan*

Plymouth, UK: Northcote House, 1994

Ryan's introduction, now somewhat out of date, though slight, is still valuable, especially for its articulation of the "moral fable" of McEwan's development as a writer, discussed in the Introduction. Peter Childs notes in *Ian McEwan's Enduring Love* that Ryan is completing work on a second edition, which will be a welcome addition from an astute McEwan critic. The first edition, like Slay's book, ends with *Black Dogs*, and features close readings with no discernible theoretical lens. Ryan's thesis is that McEwan's texts are bound together by "their power to unseat our moral certainties and sap our confidence in snap judgements" (5)—a insight that remains relevant to the later work.

CHAPTERS IN BOOKS

Gauthier, Tim S. "*Black Dogs:* Ian McEwan's Post-Holocaust Anxiety", in *Narrative Desire and Historical Reparations: A.S. Byatt, Ian McEwan, Salman Rushdie* (New York and London: Routledge, 2006) 83–131. This extensive and thoughtful treatment of *Black Dogs* contextualizes the work in relation to two of Britain's other top writers of historiographic metafiction, and provides useful theoretical background from Dominick LaCapra, Theodor Adorno and others. Working from the concept of "generalized post-Holocaust anxiety" (84), Gauthier focuses on Jeremy as an embodiment of non-Jewish society, including McEwan himself, accepting its complicity in anti-Semitic atrocities and acknowledging the potential for future recurrences. The key to this acceptance, according to Gauthier, is the act of narrating, which, while inherently flawed and unstable relative to historical truth, "bridges the past and present" (94) such that the subject acquires "a moral framework whereby the moral value of events can be endorsed or contested" (83). Jeremy's narration thus serves as a form of cultural "atonement" that may be "a preliminary to prevention" (92) through the recognition of culpability. An interesting comparison with Gauthier's argument would be the failure of narration to exculpate the past as presented in *Atonement*.

Seaboyer, Judith. "Ian McEwan: Contemporary Realism and the Novel of Ideas", in James Acheson and Sarah C.E. Ross (eds.) *The Contemporary British Novel* (Edinburgh: Edinburgh UP, 2005) 23–34. In this brief essay, Seaboyer discusses how McEwan's "fine-tuned ethical sense" and "sense of political urgency" (23) place his work in the tradition of the English realist novel of ideas, as written by authors such as George Eliot. "Realism", as Seaboyer rightly notes, is a slippery term to define, and its deployment in literary terms is often complicated by elements from other modes or genres, such as the speculative, fantasy elements in *The Child in Time* and the use of mythological symbols in *Black Dogs*. Most importantly for Seaboyer, though, realist texts treat the "private sphere" as "a way of addressing broader social and political issues" (24). Seaboyer's definition helps to undo the false binary at the heart of much of the critical reflection on McEwan's work; even in his most "private" narratives, such as the early stories, there is always an implicit social critique at play, just as there is an intensely intimate side to his most clearly political and social texts.

JOURNAL ARTICLES

Edwards, Paul. "Time, Romanticism, Modernism and Moderation in Ian McEwan's *The Child in Time*", *English: The Journal of the English Association* 44(178) (Spring 1995) 41–55. Edwards relates the unusual temporal experiences in *The Child in Time* to the Romantic poetics of William Wordsworth and modernist experimentation with form inspired by Henri Bergson's conception of *durée*. Beginning with a discussion of Stephen's journey by train to visit Julie at the cottage, itself a figural act of moving back in time to childhood, Edwards interweaves McEwan's scene with a reading of Philip Larkin's poem "The Whitsun Weddings" to arrive at an analysis of the complex role of nature in *The Child in Time*. The wheat field traversed by Stephen, he explains, is both a sign of nature subordinated to commercial needs, and an entry into a metaphysical realm that creates for Steven an existential experience more powerful than the oppressive political structure in which he lives.

James, David. "A boy stepped out": migrancy, visuality and the mapping of masculinities in later fiction of Ian McEwan, *Textual Practice* 17(1) (2003) 81–100. Focusing on *The Child in Time*, *The Innocent* and *Atonement*, James examines how McEwan's ironic and self-referential narration helps to make visible the contours of masculinity, which normally go unseen as being neutral and natural. For James, McEwan's representation of changing masculinities depends not simply on verisimilar depictions of men in various roles, but more complexly on a realist technique rife with "calculatedly ironic strategies" (90) that leave "the contradictions of McEwan's (often male) narrators/focalizers open to interrogation from a critical distance" (84). This "wryly metafictional practice," he claims, "implicat[es] the reader as [the novels] shift between ironic and complicit readings" (86). This challenging, highly theoretical article prompts readers to look more carefully at McEwan's narrational style as a vehicle for gender critique that sometimes works in tension with the texts' obvious representations of men.

Morrison, Jago. "Narration and Unease in Ian McEwan's Later Fiction", *Critique* 42(3) (Spring 2001) 253–68. Morrison examines the relationship between time, narrative and gender in *Black Dogs* and *Enduring Love*, two novels "which center on the epistemological and existential problems of masculinity" (261). He argues that narration in McEwan's fiction eschews the "linearity, control, and obsessionality" (267) associated with masculinist views of time, and instead conveys a more "feminine", fluid conception of temporality in prose that reveals its "own instability and unease" (268). In *Enduring Love*, the failure of masculinist structures is visible in Joe's frustrated attempts to contain Jed within "the public narratives of science, medicine, and law that are supposed to constitute and to defend [Joe's] embattled masculinity" (255). In *Black Dogs*, the power of June's mythical and even dream-like relationship to the past disrupts Bernard's effort to create a linear and ordered history, and moves Jeremy's memoir towards a more "feminine" narrative form.

Roger, Angela. "Ian McEwan's Portrayal of Women", *Forum for Modern Language Studies* 32(1) (1996) 11–26. This important article deals with the key issue of gender in a number of McEwan's texts, the most recent being *Black Dogs*. Roger rejects the notion of women's complicity in their own subjugation and takes issue with McEwan's feminist credentials; she argues that while there is a gradual shift in his work "from portraying women as vulnerable and defeated to women as powerful and successful," his "women characters are given objective existence in a man's world and their characterisation is a male construct of their womanhood. Interest in them is essentially in their 'otherness' from men, but this 'otherness' is seen from a man's point of view" (23, 11). McEwan's often conventionally feminized representations of women have led Roger to complain that "all of McEwan's female characters are portrayed as possessing attributes of creativity, sensibility, mystery and participation with nature, in counterpoint to the men who are, in general, portrayed as destructive, insensitive, brutal and exploitative" (25). Certainly, there are plenty of unsavory male characters in McEwan's fiction, including the composers Clive Linley and Charles Frieth in *Amsterdam* and *For You* (2008), the recently released libretto, respectively. But there are also a number of men in McEwan's texts who either learn to overcome their masculine egotism, such as Stephen in *The Child in Time*, or who have already elements of feminine nurturing, what Carol Gilligan calls "the ethics of justice and care" (63), including Jeremy in *Black Dogs* and, to a lesser extent, Henry Perowne in *Saturday*. And when Roger wrote in 1996 that "neither before nor since [*The Imitation Game*] has McEwan tried to get inside the mind of a woman character or even to create a well-rounded character" (11), she of course did not have knowledge of McEwan's plan to focalize an entire novel through the mind of a female writer, in

Atonement. Whether or not one accepts as valid Roger's critique that McEwan's treatment of women in his early fiction as itself patriarchal, it is clear that he wants to bring our attention as readers to the devastating consequences when any individual—male or female, adult or child—fails to recognize the separate needs of others and imposes their own desires upon them.

Seaboyer, Judith. "Sadism Demands a Story: Ian McEwan's *The Comfort of Strangers*", *Modern Fiction Studies* 45(4) (1999) 957–86. Using Kaja Silverman's description of patriarchy as a "dominant fiction" (957) under pressure from feminism, Seaboyer reads *The Comfort of Strangers* from a psychoanalytic perspective, revealing how the city in the novel is an unmappable labyrinth that serves as "a kind of museum" (960) for patriarchal culture, an Lacanian Imaginary correlative of the complex relationship between men and women involving sadism, masochism and desire. Seaboyer charts the "doublings and echoes" (962) of *Death in Venice* that permeate McEwan's text, noting how McEwan adapts Thomas Mann's classic modernist novel for his own purposes of exploring the concealed aspects of contemporary culture. Seaboyer's intricate theoretical argument is enhanced by a close attention to textual detail and intertextual connections.

Wallace, Elizabeth Kowaleski. "Postcolonial melancholia in Ian McEwan's *Saturday*", *Studies in the Novel* 39(4) (Winter 2007) 465–80. Drawing on Paul Gilroy's *Postcolonial Melancholia*, Wallace reads *Saturday* as a post-imperial novel in which Henry Perowne's disengagement from the multicultural society around him is symptomatic of a larger cultural malaise: "the shock and anxiety that followed from the loss of any sense that the national collective was bound by a coherent and distinctive culture" (Gilroy qtd. in Wallace 266). In this reading, Perowne serves as the symbol of Britain coming to terms with the decline of the postcolonial period while resisting the transition to a contemporary multicultural society in which anglophile traditions are rapidly turning to relics from another age. The narrative sleight-of-hand that puts us as readers directly into contact with Perowne's thoughts, which seem to brook no questioning of his cultural superiority, prompts Wallace to adopt a "politics of reading that not only actively resists the formal integrity of the novel," but also opens a space for the text to engage its audience in a reflection on the "key transitional moment" (467) of the political context in which it is set. I am wholly in agreement with Wallace's pinpointing of irony as the linchpin of the novel's political efficacy. The penetrability of the text's ironic narrative structure and allegorical coding is central to its reception, which frequently becomes fixated on aesthetic beauty to the detriment of action, much like Baxter's dreamy response to "Dover Beach".

OTHER TEXTS BY MCEWAN

The Daydreamer (London: Jonathan Cape, 1994)—The author's book of children's stories, about a boy named Peter Fortune who undergoes magical transformations, has "the imagination itself" (xv) as its subject matter, as McEwan notes in the Preface.

Introduction to *What We Believe But Cannot Prove* (New York: Harper, 2006) (xiii–xvii)—McEwan reflects on the imaginative side of science, in a volume of short essays by world-renowned scientists invited to speculate on what they think is true though not currently provable.

READINGS RELATED TO SPECIFIC TEXTS BY MCEWAN

The Cement Garden: Julian Gloag, *Our Mother's House* (1963).

The Comfort of Strangers: Thomas Mann, *Death in Venice* (1924).

The Child in Time: Christian Hardyment, Dream Babies: *Three Centuries of Good Advice on Childcare* (1983).

Enduring Love: Steven Pinker, *The Language Instinct* (1994).

Amsterdam: Albert Camus, *The Fall* (1956).

Atonement: Lucilla Andrews (1977); *No Time for Romance*; Jane Austen, *Northanger Abbey* (1803); Elizabeth Bowen, *The Heat of the Day* (1949).

Saturday: Saul Bellow, *Herzog* (1964); James Joyce, *Ulysses* (1922); Virginia Woolf, *Mrs Dalloway* (1925).

On Chesil Beach: John Fowles, *The French Lieutenant's Woman* (1969).

READINGS ON ETHICAL PHILOSOPHY AND ETHICS IN LITERATURE

Bauman, Zygmunt. *Postmodern Ethics* (Oxford: Blackwell, 1993).

Booth, Wayne C. *The Company We Keep: An Ethics of Fiction* (Berkeley and Los Angeles: University of California Press, 1998).

Champagne, Roland A. *The Ethics of Reading According to Emmanuel Lévinas* (Amsterdam: Rodopi, 1998).

Eaglestone, Robert. *Ethical Criticism: Reading After Lévinas* (Edinburgh: Edinburgh University Press, 1997).

Karnicky, Jeffrey. *Contemporary Fiction and the Ethics of Modern Culture* (New York: Palgrave Macmillan, 2007).

Miller, J. Hillis. *The Ethics of Reading: Kant, de Man, Eliot, Trollope, James and Benjamin* (New York: Columbia University Press, 1987).

Newton, Adam Zachary. *Narrative Ethics* (Cambridge: Harvard University Press, 1995).

Nussbaum, Martha. *Love's Knowledge: Essays on Philosophy and Literature* (New York: Oxford University Press, 1990).

Rorty, Richard. *Contingency, Irony and Solidarity* (Cambridge: Cambridge University Press, 1989).

Taylor, Charles. *Sources of the Self: The Making of the Modern Identity* (Cambridge: Cambridge University Press, 1989).

BIBLIOGRAPHY

MAJOR TEXTS BY MCEWAN (EDITIONS USED)

Amsterdam (Toronto: Vintage, 1999).
Atonement (Toronto: Knopf Canada, 2001).
Black Dogs (Toronto: Vintage, 1993).
The Cement Garden (New York: Random House, 2003).
The Child in Time (Toronto: Lester & Orpen Dennys, 1987).
The Comfort of Strangers (London: Vintage, 1997).
The Daydreamer (Toronto: Doubleday Canada, 1994).
Enduring Love (Toronto: Vintage Canada, 1997).
First Love, Last Rites (New York: Anchor, 2003).
For You: The Libretto for Michael Berkeley's Opera (London: Vintage, 2008).
The Imitation Game and Other Plays (Boston: Houghton Mifflin, 1982).
In Between the Sheets (New York: Anchor, 2003).
The Innocent (Toronto: Key Porter, 2002).
A Move Abroad (London: Picador, 1989).
On Chesil Beach (Toronto: Alfred A. Knopf, 2007).
Saturday (Toronto: Alfred A. Knopf, 2005).
Soursweet (London and Boston: Faber, 1988).

ARTICLES BY MCEWAN (CITED); FOR A COMPLETE LIST, SEE IANMCEWAN.COM

"Beyond Belief" (2001), available online at http://www.ianmcewan.com/bib/articles/9-11-02.html
"How could we have forgotten that this was always going to happen?", *The Guardian* (8 July 2005), available online at http://www.guardian.co.uk/world/2005/jul/08/terrorism.july74
"Mother Tongue" (October 2001), available online at http://www.ianmcewan.com/bib/articles/mother-tongue.html
"Only Love and Then Oblivion" (2001), available online at http://www.ianmcewan.com/bib/articles/love-oblivion.html
"Save the boot room, save the Earth", *The Guardian* (19 March 2005), available online at http://www.guardian.co.uk/artanddesign/2005/mar/19/art1

OTHER WORKS CITED

Alvarez, Al. "It Happened One Night", *New York Review of Books*, 54.12 (19 July 2007), 1–4, available online at http://www.nybooks.com/articles/20394

Associated Press. "McEwan Happy with 'Atonement' Film" (27 September 2008), available online at http://www.cbsnews.com/stories/2008/02/12/entertainment/main3820525.shtml?source=R

Auden, W.H. "In Memory of W.B. Yeats (d. Jan. 1939)", in Edward Mendelson (ed.), *Collected Poems* (New York: Random House, 1976), 197–8.

Bachelard, Gaston. *The Poetics of Space* (New York: Orion, 1964).

Begley, Adam. "The Art of Fiction CLXXIII" [Interview with Ian McEwan], *Paris Review* (Summer 2002), 31–60.

Benjamin, Jessica. *The Bonds of Love: Psychoanalysis, Feminism and the Problem of Domination* (New York: Pantheon, 1988).

Bloechl, Jeffrey. *The Face of the Other and the Trace of God: Essays on the Philosophy of Emmanuel Lévinas* (New York: Fordham University Press, 2000).

Bold Type. [Interview with Ian McEwan], available online at http://www.randomhouse.com/boldtype/1298/mcewan/interview.html

Byatt, A.S. *Possession: A Romance* (New York: Random House, 1990).

Cassirer, Ernst. *The Philosophy of Symbolic Forms: Volume Two: Mythical Thought*. Ralph Manheim (trans.) (New Haven and London: Yale University Press, 1955).

Childs, Peter. " 'Believing is seeing': The eye of the beholder", in Peter Childs (ed.) *McEwan's Enduring Love* (London and New York: Routledge, 2007), 107–21.

——. *Ian McEwan's* Enduring Love (London and New York: Routledge, 2007).

——. (ed.). *The Fiction of Ian McEwan: A Reader's Guide to the Essential Criticism* (London: Palgrave Macmillan, 2006).

Chotiner, Isaac. " 'Atonement' author Ian McEwan on Bellow, the Internet, atheism, and why his books are still scary" [Interview with Ian McEwan], *The New Republic* (11 January 2008), available online at http://www.tnr.com/politics/story.html?id=2cee28d1-869d-447a-8e83-4e046f5ad6df

Danziger, Danny. "In Search of Two Characters", *Times* (27 June 1987), 13c.

Eberhart, John Mark. "In a better light: Ian McEwan's *Atonement* finds new readers as a paperback", *Knight Ridder/Tribune News Service* (4 June 2003), available online at http://www.accessmylibrary.com/coms2/summary_0286-6928703_ITM

Edwards, Paul. "Time, Romanticism, Modernism and Moderation in Ian McEwan's *The Child in Time*", *English: The Journal of the English Association* 44 (178) (Spring 1995), 41–55.

Ellis. "Barbaric Documents: The Politics of Ian McEwan's *Saturday*", [weblog], available online at http://barbaricdocument.blogspot.com/search?updated-min=2005-01-01T00%3A00%3A00Z&updated-max=2006-01-01T00%3A00%3A00Z&max-results=3

Felman, Shoshana. "Turning the Screw of Interpretation", in Shoshana Felman (ed.) *Literature and Psychoanalysis: The Question of Reading: Otherwise* (Baltimore and London: Johns Hopkins University Press, 1982), 94–207.

Gauthier, Tim S. "*Black Dogs*: Ian McEwan's Post-Holocaust Anxiety", in *Narrative Desire and Historical Reparations: A.S. Byatt, Ian McEwan, Salman Rushdie* (New York and London: Routledge, 2006), 83–131.

Gilligan, Carol. *In a Different Voice: Psychological Theory and Women's Development* (Cambridge: Harvard University Press, 1983).

Haffenden, John. [Interview with Ian McEwan], *Novelists in Interview* (London and New York: Methuen, 1985), 168–90.

Hamilton, Ian. "Points of Departure" [Interview with Ian McEwan], *The New Review* 5 (2) (Autumn 1978), 9–21.

Hand, Séan. *The Lévinas Reader* (New York: Blackwell, 1989).

Hassan, Ihab. "Cities of Mind, Urban Words: The Dematerialization of Metropolis in Contemporary American Fiction", in Michael C. Jaye and Ann Chalmers Watts (eds) *Literature and the Urban Experience: Essays on the City and Literature* (New Brunswick, New Jersey: Rutgers University Press, 1981), 93–112.

Head, Dominic. *Ian McEwan* (Manchester and New York: Manchester University Press, 2007).

Hoyle, Ben. "McEwan hits back at call for atonement", *Times Online* (27 November 2006), available online at http://business.timesonline.co.uk/tol/business/law/public_law/ article650961.ece

Hutcheon, Linda. *Irony's Edge: The Theory and Politics of Irony* (New York and London: Routledge, 1994).

——. *A Poetics of Postmodernism: History, Theory, Fiction* (New York and London: Routledge, 1988).

James, David. " 'A boy stepped out': migrancy, visuality, and the mapping of masculinities in later fiction of Ian McEwan", *Textual Practice* 17 (1) (2003), 81–100.

Knights, Ben. *Writing Masculinities: Male Narratives in Twentieth-Century Fiction* (London: Macmillan, 1999).

Koval, Ramona. [Interview with Ian McEwan], *Erudition* (4 April 2004), available online at http://www.eruditiononline.com/04.04/ian_mcewan.htm

Le Corbusier (Charles-Édouard Jeanneret-Gris). *The Radiant City* (Paris: Vincent, Freal, 1964).

Lefebvre, Henri. *The Production of Space*. Donald Nicholson-Smith (trans.) (Oxford: Blackwell, 1991).

Lévinas, Emmanuel. *Collected Philosophical Papers*. Alphonso Lingis (trans.) (Pittsburgh: Duquesne University Press, 1998).

——. *Entre Nous* (New York: Columbia University Press, 1998).

——. *Totality and Infinity*. Alphonso Lingis (trans.) (Pittsburgh: Duquesne University Press, 1969).

Malcolm, David. *Understanding Ian McEwan* (Columbia: University of South Carolina Press, 2002).

Mars-Jones, Adam. "I think I'm right, therefore I am", *The Observer* (7 September 1999), available online at http://www.guardian.co.uk/books/1999/sep/07/fiction.reviews.print

——. *Venus Envy* (London: Chatto & Windus, 1990).

Matthews, Sean. "Seven types of unreliability", in Peter Childs (ed.) *Ian McEwan's* Enduring Love (London and New York: Routledge, 2007), 92–106.

Mellor, Anne K. "Why Women Didn't Like Romanticism", in Gene W. Ruoff (ed.) *The Romantics and Us: Essays on Literature and Culture* (New Brunswick and London: Rutgers University Press, 1990), 274–87.

Miller, J. Hillis. *Reading Narrative* (Norman: University of Oklahoma Press, 1998).

Miller, Laura. "Ian McEwan fools British shrinks", *Salon Books* (21 September 1999), available online at http://www.salon.com/books/log/1999/09/21/mcewan

Morrison, Jago. "Narration and Unease in Ian McEwan's Later Fiction", *Critique* 42 (3) (Spring 2001), 253–68.

Morrison, Richard. "Opera gets between the sheets with Ian McEwan's For You." *Times Online* (9 May 2008), available online at http://entertainment.timesonline.co.uk/tol/art_and_entertainment/stage/opera/article3894802.ece

Noakes, Jonathan and Margaret Reynolds. [Interview with Ian McEwan], in Jonathan Noakes and Margaret Reynolds (eds) *Ian McEwan* (London: Vintage, 2002), 10–23.

Out of the Book Production. *Ian McEwan: On Chesil Beach* (DVD, 2007).

Pifer, Ellen. *Demon or Doll: Images of the Child in Contemporary Writing and Culture* (Charlottesville and London: University Press of Virginia, 2000).

Pile, Steve. *The Body and the City: Psychoanalysis, Space and Subjectivity* (London and New York: Routledge, 1996).

Popham, Peter. "'I despise Islamism': Ian McEwan faces backlash over press interview", *The Independent* (22 June 2008), available online at http://www.independent.co.uk/news/world/europe/i-despise-islamism-ian-mcewan-faces-backlash-over-press-interview-852030.html

Pritchett, V.S. "Shredded Novels: *In Between the Sheets*", *New York Review of Books* (24 January 1980), 31–2.

Ricks, Christopher. "Adolescence and After", [Interview with Ian McEwan], *Listener* (12 April 1979), 526–7.

Roger, Angela. "Ian McEwan's Portrayal of Women", *Forum for Modern Language Studies* 32 (1) (1996), 11–26.

Ryan, Kiernan. "After the fall", in Peter Childs (ed.) *Ian McEwan's* Enduring Love (London and New York: Routledge, 2007), 44–54.

———. *Ian McEwan* (Plymouth: Northcote House, 1994).

Schemberg, Claudia. *Achieving "At-one-ment": Storytelling and the Concept of the Self in Ian McEwan's* The Child in Time, Black Dogs, Enduring Love, *and* Atonement (Frankfurt: Peter Lang, 2004).

Seaboyer, Judith. "Ian McEwan: Contemporary Realism and the Novel of Ideas", in James Acheson and Sarah C.E. Ross (eds) *The Contemporary British Novel* (Edinburgh: Edinburgh University Press, 2005), 23–34.

———. "Sadism Demands a Story: Ian McEwan's *The Comfort of Strangers*", *Modern Fiction Studies* 45 (4) (1999), 957–86.

Siegel, Lee. "The Imagination of Disaster", *The Nation* (11 April 2005): 33–34, available online at http://www.thenation.com/doc/20050411/siegel

Slay, Jr, Jack. *Ian McEwan* (New York: Twayne, 1996).

Solomon, Deborah. "A Sinner's Tale" [Interview with Ian McEwan], *New York Times Magazine* (2 December 2007), available online at http://www.nytimes.com/2007/12/02/magazine/02wwln-Q4-t.html

Spence, Donald. "Narrative Recursion", in Shlomith Rimmon-Kenan (ed.) *Discourse in Psychoanalysis and Literature* (London and New York: Methuen, 1987), 188–210.

Wallace, Elizabeth Kowaleski. "Postcolonial melancholia in Ian McEwan's *Saturday*", *Studies in the Novel* 39 (4) (Winter 2007), 465–80.

Wells, Lynn. *Allegories of Telling: Self-Referential Narrative in Contemporary British Fiction* (Amsterdam and Atlanta: Rodopi, 2003).

Whitney, Helen. "Faith and Doubt at Ground Zero", [Interview with Ian McEwan], *Frontline* (April 2002), available online at http://www.pbs.org/wgbh/pages/frontline/shows/faith/interviews/mcewan.html

Woods, Tim. "The Ethical Subject: The Philosophy of Emmanuel Levinas", in Karl Simms (ed.) *Ethics and the Subject* (Amsterdam and Atlanta: Rodopi, 1997), 53–60.

Žižek, Slavoj. "Two Ways to Avoid the Real of Desire", in *Looking Awry: An Introduction to Jacques Lacan through Popular Culture* (Cambridge, Massachusetts: MIT Press, 1991), 48–66.

———. *The Sublime Object of Ideology* (London and New York: Verso, 1989).

———. "The Truth Arises from Misrecognition", in Ellie Ragland-Sullivan and Mark Bracher (eds) *Lacan and the Subject of Language* (New York and London: Routledge, 1991), 188–212.

INDEX